# Marriage God's Way
# Model Marriage

## DR. CHINWE BENEDICTA OKONKWO - PHD

authorHOUSE®

*AuthorHouse™*
*1663 Liberty Drive*
*Bloomington, IN 47403*
*www.authorhouse.com*
*Phone: 833-262-8899*

*Published by AuthorHouse 07/29/2023*

*ISBN: 979-8-8230-0679-8 (sc)*
*ISBN: 979-8-8230-0678-1 (e)*

*Library of Congress Control Number: 2023910949*

# CONTENTS

# ACKNOWLEDGEMENTS

I hereby appreciate the Source of my being, the unseen hands that successfully move and direct my destiny in spite of the vicissitudes and chains of aggravated circumstances that attempted to scuttle my ambition in life. I give God all the glory.

First and foremost, I hereby render due respect and honour to my Creator and my Saviour, the Most High God, the Author and Finisher of my faith, who gave me the inspiration and wisdom to put my spiritual ideas in writing. May the name of the Almighty God be supremely glorified.

Oh, to my invaluable, precious and priceless parents, with deep sense of regard and high esteem to my highly beloved parents; I am very much grateful to my sweet, beloved and cherished mother of the blessed memory, late Mrs. Josephine Nwoye Okonkwo, whose untimely demise created an indelible wound and a constant vacuum in my life. You were indeed a Priceless Jewel.

With deep sense of regard and appreciation to my beloved father, late chief Honourable Commissioner John Nwankwo Paul Okonkwo, former Commissioner, Civil Service Commission, Old Anambra State, former Deputy Registrar of Cooperatives, Old Anambra State, former University Lecturer, author of several University text-books, former First National President, Association of Cooperative Professionals of Nigeria, former First President, Cooperative Federation of New Anambra State, First Vice-President, Nigerian Agricultural Cooperative Marketing Organization, member, National Committee on Cooperative Research and Development, former President General of Igbo-ukwu Development Union (IDU), Igbo-ukwu in Aguata Local Government Area of Anambra State, Nigeria, with his traditional title of "Ojenanwayo" 1 of Igbo-ukwu.

Also, former chairman of Igbo-ukwu Development Union (IDU), Enugu branch, Enugu, Old Anambra State Nigeria for many years.

# DEDICATION

This book is dedicated to God the Father, the Son, and the Holy Spirit who is the institutor of marriage.

# PREFACE

# What Is Christian Marriage?

It may be defined as the union of one Christian man to one Christian woman for life. But my favourite definition is this one:

Christian marriage is "a total commitment and a total sharing of the total person with another person until death." In a Christian marriage, "the dependence is mutual, the obligation reciprocal, and the dependence on God, absolute." At the heart of marriage is companionship, communion and consummation. God's blue- print for marriage involves Leaving, Cleaving and Becoming One Flesh.

Marriage is two people becoming one; liabilities and assets becoming one.

The husband and wife relationship is the closest, the most intimate of all human relationships for it is likened to the relationship between Christ and the Church **(Ephesians 5:22- 33).**

The number of failed marriages in the church is very alarming. Marriage is 100% spiritual, is God's idea, not man's idea. If you must do marriage well, you must do it from God, do it from God's Word. Let the Bible be your watch, let the Bible guide you. God is the originator of marriage.

Marriage was the first institution God really started.

When God made Adam and Eve, the first thing He started was marriage.

God's design for the family can be seen in the first family **(Genesis 2:18-24; 4:1-2).**

Marriage is a permanent relationship as attested by the Words of our Lord Jesus, **What therefore God hath joined together, let not man put asunder** (Matthew 19:6b, Mark 10:9).

It is also intended to be a harmonious partnership**. And they twain shall be one flesh** (Matthew 19:6a, Mark 10:8a).

Furthermore, it is for spiritual companionship**: Can two walk together, except they be agreed** (Amos 3:3).

The reason why there are so many problems and divorces in marriages these days is because, their principles are based on societal and cultural backgrounds of individuals.

These principles have also found their ways into Christian homes too, because, there are not enough grounded and established teachings about marriage in our churches.

It is astonishing these days that people who are old enough to marry and have children, now choose not to marry, but live as single parents and the law approves it as normal.

Since there is such a breakdown of what marriage really is, we now have epidemic outbreak of all kinds of sexual diseases and new definitions of what marriage is supposed to be. For example, lesbianism (women in love with women), and gay (men in love with men) now have rights in some places in the world to marry legally in churches and courts.

To revive marriage institution, church of Jesus Christ must clearly define, teach, preach and practise marriage as God ordained it. It must be openly defined; not as if it is a sin to preach about marriage in our churches. God is the initiator of marriage.

This book presents a Scriptural understanding of the roles of the man, woman and children in the home.

The book is aimed to introduce a new perspective in the quest of stemming divorces, unhappy homes and their devastations on all concerned men, women and children. You may call it preventive counselling and mentoring. It is also a reference- a useful one for those in marriage and going through difficult situations.

A marriage is a blending that should last; and a home should be the happiest place on earth- not a hell.

Preparation for a happy home begins before you get married. A society with happy homes is a happy society and nation.

This book will help singles; it teaches young men and women how to search for their life partners.

If you want your marriage to prosper, start making adjustments in your marriage from the things you will learn in this book.

James 1:22 says, we should be hearers and doers of the Word, and Jesus said in John 8:31, that if we abide in His teachings, then we become true disciples.

Read, study and apply the principles in this book, and become one of those who will stand in the Word of God to revive the marriage institution in our society.

Dr. Chi B. Okonkwo- Ph.D.

# CHAPTER ONE

# Why God Created Marriage?

## SEVEN PURPOSES OF MARRIAGE

1. Companionship- Nobody is an island, you need somebody. Ecclesiastes 4:11: **Again, if two lie together, then they have heat: but how can one be warm alone**? The first principal reason for Christian marriage is for mutual fellowship. Loneliness is not good. It is dangerous. The Lord saw the man needed companionship, hence, the creation of woman. **Genesis 2:18-22, 24**. There is nothing like having somebody. There are exceptions according to Apostle Paul in **1 Corinthians 7:32**.

   **Ecclesiastes 4: 11: Again, if two lie together, then they have heat: but how can one be warm alone**?

2. **Complementary-**To complement mankind- to complement each other. You do not have everything. Two are better than one because they have a good reward for their efforts and endeavours. **Genesis 2:18: And the LORD God said, It is not good that the man should be alone; I will make him an help meet for him.**

   **Ecclesiastes 4:9-12:**

   **Two are better than one; because they have a good reward for their labour.**

   **For if they fall, the one will lift up his fellow: but woe to him that is alone when he falleth; for he hath not another to help him up.**

Again, if two lie together, then they have heat: but how can one be warm alone?

And if one prevail against him, two shall withstand him; and a threefold cord is not quickly broken.

When people come together, they can help each other.

One will chase one thousand, and two put ten thousand to flight **(Deuteronomy 32:30).**

**Deuteronomy 32:30: How should one chase a thousand, and two put ten thousand to flight, except their Rock had sold them, and the LORD had shut them up?**

**In Genesis 2:18: And the LORD God said, It is not good that the man should be alone; I will make him an help meet for him.**

3. **Coitus (Sexual relationship)** – Marriage was created for sex, for meeting our sexual needs. God made us with sexual desires that are good, holy and legitimate but must only be satisfied in marriage. This will also check the sinful life of adultery or fornication **(1 Corinthians 7:2).**

**First Corinthians 7:2-5, 9: Nevertheless, to avoid fornication, let every man have his own wife, and let every woman have her own husband.**

**Let the husband render unto the wife due benevolence: and likewise also the wife unto the husband.**

**The wife hath not power of her own body, but the husband: and likewise also the husband hath not power of his own body, but the wife.**

**Defraud ye not one the other, except it be with consent for a time, that ye may give yourselves to fasting and prayer; and come together again, that Satan tempt you not for your incontinency.**

**But if they cannot contain, let them marry: for it is better to marry than to burn.**

**Proverbs 5:19: Let her be as the loving hind and pleasant roe; let her breasts satisfy thee at all times; and be thou ravished always with her love.**

Paul said instead of burning, marry. The Bible says, even if you want to fast, you must obtain consent from your partner. Your body is not your own. When either of the partner needs sex, the other partner must submit, not only when two of you need it. Is wrong to deprive your partner sex, you are defrauding your partner if his or her sexual needs are not met.

4. **Procreation**- For having children. God said in **Malachi 2,** that the reason He created marriage is to have godly seeds. To raise godly children within the marriage context.

   Parenting is not only for women, but both of you. Your children will learn more from how you live. Do not insult your spouse in the presence of your children.

   To obey the command of God, which is to be fruitful, multiply, propagate the human race and replenish the earth through child bearing/rearing in the fear of God **(Genesis 1:28; 9:1; Proverbs 22:6).**

   **Genesis 1:28: And God blessed them, and God said unto them, Be fruitful, and multiply, and replenish the earth, and subdue it: and have dominion over the fish of the sea, and over the fowl of the air, and over every living thing that moveth upon the earth.**

5. **Covenant Relationship**- God has covenant relationship, not normal relationship. Covenant relationship, this person shall give me all I need. In Mathematics, one plus one is two, but in marriage, one plus one is one. For reliability and stability. Somebody has pledged to be with you all your life. Marriage is unlimited sharing.

6. **Character Development**- Marriage develops your character. Marriage trains you.

   Marriage builds your character.

7. **Collaboration**- Two are better than one. **Ecclesiastes 4:9: Two are better than one; because they have a good reward for their labour.**

   **Matthew 18:19:" Again I say unto you, That if two of you shall agree on earth as touching anything that they shall ask, it shall be done for them of my Father which is in heaven".**

   It takes two (a man and a woman) to make "one flesh" **(Genesis 2:24).**

   To accelerate their result.

# THE RIGHT CHOICE IN MARRIAGE

God still chooses the right marriage partner for His children who are willing to trust and obey him. Psalm 25:9 says: **The meek will he guide in judgement: and the meek will he teach his way.**

Judgement in the above Scripture means decision- making or preference, thus, it is saying, God will guide the meek in making choices. Even if you have basic knowledge in the area where you have to make a choice, you still need to depend on God.

Read 2 Corinthians 6:14, and 1 Kings 11:1-11.

Apart from the choice of whom to serve, the choice of a life partner in marriage is another fundamental decision that can affect a person's destiny positively or negatively. Wrong choice in marriage may override the choice to serve God. Solomon chose to marry many strange women and they influenced him to forsake God and serve idols. The choice of a life partner will go to a very large extent in either strengthening or weakening a person's relationship with God. Solomon did not want to forget God who had done so much for him, but his choice of wives caused him to err.

Many people make costly mistakes because they do not seek God's guidance. No matter how much you know, depending on God in making a choice is a sign of meekness and humility. God still chooses the right marriage partner for His children who are willing to trust and obey Him. Psalm 25:9 says: **The meek will he guide in judgement and the meek will he teach his way.**

Judgement in the above Scripture means decision- making or preference, thus, it is saying God will guide the meek in making choices. Even if you have basic knowledge in the area where you have to make a choice, you still need to depend on God. Lot chose a piece of land that he knew would be very good for agriculture. He surveyed the land, assessed its prospects, knew it would sufficiently support animal husbandry and thus, chose to relocate there. His knowledge was good, but it was limited, because, he did not know what the future held for that land. God eventually destroyed the land in the overthrow of Sodom and Gomorrah (Genesis 13:9-11). There appears to be nothing wrong in Lot making a choice, however, his mistake was that he did not seek God's guidance. Relying solely on one's knowledge can ruin such a person's destiny and lead to eternal damnation.

This is why Proverbs 31:30 says: **Favour is deceitful, and beauty is vain: but a woman that feareth the LORD, she shall be praised.**

Seek the face of God and sound Christian counselling before choosing a life partner. Do not choose by sight and human knowledge alone, God's guidance is key to making the best choice in all that concern you.

## MISTAKES TO AVOID BEFORE MARRIAGE

1.  Do not marry a man who has no job.

    Before God gave Adam Eve, God gave him a job. He said, this is the garden, keep the garden. No income do not marry him. Go and get a job first. Man should provide for the family not the other way round.

    Proverbs 31:30 says, **Favour is deceitful, and beauty is vain: but a woman that feareth the LORD, she shall be praised.** Do not marry Delilah for the sake of beauty. Delilah stopped Sampson.

2.  Do not marry outside the church.

    I tell you point- blank, is better to be single than marry a devil. Do not marry and think you can change him. Goliath was tall he lost his head. If the person does not change before marriage, he will not change. King Saul was handsome, he lost his crown. If not a child of God, do not associate with him. Delilah was beautiful but she stopped Sampson. Do not unequally yoke with unbeliever. Ask him if he believes in holiness.

3.  Do not marry a girl who is lazy.

    If she is lazy as a single girl, how could she cope with the children? A girl who cannot cook will not be a good wife you have to eat in your house. Colossians 3:1-3.

    Marry someone who looks differently from others that people will copy, not someone who copies others. If he says nobody is perfect, only God, run, ask him if he believes in holiness.

4.  Do not marry a girl simply because she can sing.

    God loves worshippers. The devil was a choir master in heaven. There are some fallen angels. Marry a prayer warrior. Is better to be single than to marry the wrong fellow, you start your hell on earth. I pray that who has already married, God will change the wrong to right. Those who have not married at all, let God direct you to marry the right person, in Jesus' name. First Samuel 16:14 to end. When demon was tormenting king Saul, David was brought to sing for Saul, and the demons went away. David wrote a lot of Psalms. Music is important, right music, wrong music can invite demons. Number one reason why God chose David to be king, because, he was a musician singing the right kind of songs.

Joshua 1:1-9, Num.14:27-31

Moses failed to take the people to the promised land, Moses failed, Joshua did not. You will take over, there is a proviso, provided you do not fail the foundation. Deuteronomy 34:9. Moses laid the foundation. You have to hold the foundation built by your fore fathers. A ministry does not stand until at least there is one transition, a successful successor. Do not play with your foundation. The elders are the foundations, the youths are followers. If you remain connected to your root, you will never dry up. Joshua 7, God said to Joshua, nobody can stop you. Saul failed, but David did not. King Saul forgot his Source, he dried up, when he forgot the person who gave him the Source, he dried up.

5.  Do not marry a girl who is worldly. I am believing God when you marry, you will marry the right person.

# CHOOSE A QUALITY HOME

Before you decide to get married, you must make sure you find out as much as possible about your potential spouse. This was the practice in the olden days. The elders did an investigative research on the potential spouse and his/her family background before giving their consent from their findings. Was this any use? Yes! Such a check can fore-stall the marriage to avoid misery in the home.

Here are some specific benefits of prior investigative enquiry before consent to marry.

## Health History

There are certain health enquiries you need to make because forewarned is forearmed. Before commitment to marry, check out the family health history on both sides. Check for:

Blood type, to ensure compatibility and to avoid S.S. phenomenon.

- Breast cancer
- Hypertension
- Depression
- Mental illness
- Diabetes
- Asthma
- HIV/AID

Your finding will prepare your mind for any emergency in the future.

## FINDINGS THAT COULD STOP A MARRIAGE FROM TAKING PLACE- BY THE TRADITIONAL ELDERS' NORMS:

Closeness in blood relationship. This is important to avoid the gene problems; and the abomination of incest. If there was a bad or very bad testimony in the family history for instance, a trait of Kleptomania, criminality, and instability of character in marriage homes especially for girls in that family.

The outdated caste label.

Pattern of longevity that is, whether they died early or lived long.

The reputation of the parents and the reputation of all the other siblings that got married- whether they were wayward; and messed around in their husbands' homes.

History of infertility, or child bearing.

The behaviour and character of children from that family- whether they were courteous and respectful.

The list can be very long; and some of their questions apparently facetious; but the essence of this prior enquiry is to ensure that it is okay for the two people involved to get married, and if not to stop them.

In the traditional setting, marriage is expected to have longevity. Divorce was rare.

We have something to learn from our fore fathers. The generational gap and its differences notwithstanding, the concept of pre-enquiry is good and acceptable, and should be applied today asking our own type of "modern" questions to pre-empt avoidable problems that could plague the home.

## DECISION FROM HELL

It is a decision from hell to settle for a single parent home because you do not want to deal with the challenges of marriage.

To start with, you are in downright disobedience to God's commandment having children outside wedlock. Your home is not a heavenly home. It is a guest house for your male consorts where they have fun and go, and get you pregnant for another child.

You think it is fun- collecting monthly stipend from different fathers of your children. It is in fact a form of child abuse.

Proper marriage and proper home require discipline, morality and submission to the pattern ordained by God.

## PRE-MARITAL SEX

Pre- marital sex is one of the hidden causes of bad marriages and unhappy homes.

God in his wisdom blessed sexual intercourse to the married couple to be fruitful and multiply; and to join together as one flesh. God did not bless sexual intercourse to "boyfriends" and "girlfriends". Outside marriage, sexual intercourse is called fornication and it is condemned by God. Fornication is a deadly sin. The Bible says, **Flee fornication, 1 Corinthians 6.:18.**

The Word of God says that marriage is honourable and the bed undefiled.

**Hebrews 13:4: Marriage is honourable in all, and the bed undefiled: but whoremongers and adulterers God will judge.**

# CHAPTER TWO

# Biblical Pathway To Finding A Life Partner

1. **Hosea**- Found and married a prostitute called Gomer.

   **Hosea 1: 1-3:**

   **THE word of the LORD that came unto Hosea, the son of**

   **Be-èri, in the days of Uz-zi´ah, Jo'tham, A'haz, and Hez-e-ki'ah, kings of Judah, and in the days of Jeroboam the son of Jo'ash, king of Israel.**

   **The beginning of the word of the LORD by Hosea. And the LORD said to Hosea, Go, take unto thee a wife of whoredoms and children of whoredoms: for the land hath committed great whoredom, departing from the LORD.**

   **So he went and took Go'mer the daughter of Dib'la-im; which conceived, and bare him a son.**

2. **Moses**- To succeed in life (therefore favoured by God, one must not only be courteous but chivalrous! Even in a foreign country where one is exposed to hostile forces. One must always stand for the right and be ready to help the weak and needy in order to be favoured by His "cooperative Will." We can find one outstanding example in the Old Testament. It is the case of Moses who defended the seven daughters of Reuel (Jethro) against marauding shepherds (Exodus 2:16,17). Moses found a man with seven daughters, watered the flock, found a wife free of charge and married.

9

Exodus 2:16-22:

NOW the priest of Mid'i-an had seven daughters: and they came and drew water, and filled the troughs to water their father's flock.

And the shepherds came and drove them away: but Moses stood up and helped them, and watered their flock.

And when they came to Reuel their father, he said, How is it that ye are come so soon today?

And they said, An Egyptian delivered us out of the hand of the shepherds, and also drew water enough for us, and watered the flock.

And he said unto his daughters, And where is he? Why is it that ye have left the man?

And Moses was content to dwell with the man: and he gave Moses Zip-po'rah his daughter.

And she bare him a son, and he called his name Ger'shom: for he said, I have been a stranger in a strange land.

3. **Boaz**- Bought an estate, a vineyard, saw a poor lady Ruth and married her.

Ruth 4: 5-10:

Then said Boaz, What day thou buyest the field of the hand of Naomi, thou must buy it also of Ruth the Moabitess, the wife of the dead, to raise up the name of the dead upon his inheritance.

And the kinsman said, I cannot redeem it for myself, lest I mar mine own inheritance: redeem thou my right to thyself; for I cannot redeem it.

NOW this was the manner in former time in Israel concerning redeeming and concerning changing, for to confirm all things; a man plucked off his shoe, and gave it to his neighbour: and this was a testimony in Israel.

Therefore the kinsman said unto Boaz, Buy it for thee. So he drew off his shoe.

And Boaz said unto the elders, and unto all the people, Ye are witnesses this day, that I have bought all that was Elimelech's, and all that was Chil'i-on's and Mah'lon's, of the hand of Na-o'mi.

Moreover Ruth the Moabitess, the wife of Mah'lon, have I purchased to be my wife, to raise up the name of the dead upon his inheritance, that the name of the dead be not cut off from among his brethren, and from the gate of his place: ye are witness this day.

4. **Benjamite-**Captured slave, stole a woman and ran away, and turned her into a wife, that was how he got a wife.

**Judges 19:25:**

But the men would not hearken to him: so the man took his concubine, and brought her forth unto them; and they knew her, and abused her all the night until the morning: and when the day began to spring, they let her go.

5. **Jacob**- Served Laban seven years for Leah, got a wrong wife, and served another seven years for Rachel being fourteen years in whole, and got the wife he wanted.

**Genesis 29: 15-31:**

And Laban said unto Jacob, Because thou art my brother, shouldest thou therefore serve me for nought? tell me, what shall thy wages be?

And Laban had two daughters: the name of the elder was Leah, and the name of the younger was Rachel.

Leah was tender eyed; but Rachel was beautiful and well favoured.

And Jacob loved Rachel; and said, I will serve thee seven years for Rachel thy younger daughter.

And Laban said, It is better that I give her to thee, than that I should give her to another man: abide with me.

And Jacob served seven years for Rachel; and they seemed unto him but a few days, for the love he had to her.

And Jacob said unto Laban, Give me my wife, for my days are fulfilled, that I may go in unto her.

And Laban gathered together all the men of the place, and made a feast. And it came to pass in the evening, that he took Leah his daughter, and brought her to him; and he went in unto her.

And Laban gave unto his daughter Leah Zilpah his maid for an handmaid.

And it came to pass, that in the morning, behold, it was Leah: and he said to Laban, What is this thou hast done unto me? did not I serve with thee for Rachel?

And Laban said, It must not be so done in our country, to give the younger before the first born.

Fulfil her week, and we will give thee this also for the service which thou shalt serve with me yet seven other years.

And Jacob did so, and fulfilled her week: and he gave him Rachel his daughter to wife also.

And Laban gave to Rachel his daughter Bilhah his handmaid to be her maid.

And he went in also unto Rachel, and he loved also Rachel more than Leah, and served with him yet seven other years.

And when the LORD saw that Leah was hated, he opened her womb: but Rachel was barren.

6. **David**- David killed Goliath, got rich, and got a wife. King Saul said whoever kills Goliath, he would enrich him, give his daughter for marriage, and be exempted from taxes.

**First Samuel 17:25:**

And the men of Israel said, Have ye seen this man that is come up? surely to defy Israel is he come up: and it shall be, that the man who killeth him, the king will enrich him with great riches, and will give him his daughter, and make his father's house free in Israel.

7. **David**- David killed Uriah and married his wife **(2 Samuel 11).**

8. **Ahasuerus**- Ahasuerus organized a beauty contest as the Bachelors do. All the virgins in the land came, he found a wife.

**Esther 2: 3-4:**

**And let the king appoint officers in all the provinces of his kingdom, that they may gather together all the fair young virgins unto Shushan the palace, to the house of the women, unto the custody of He'ge the king's chamberlain, keeper of the women; and let their things for purification be given them:**

**And let the maiden which pleaseth the king be queen instead of Vashti. And the thing pleased the king; and he did so.**

9. **Solomon**- Married seven hundred wives and three hundred concubines, one thousand women to himself in order to be faithful.

**First Kings 11: 1-3:**

**BUT king Solomon loved many strange women, together with the daughter of Pharaoh, women of the Moabites, Ammonites, Edomites, Zidonians, and Hittites; Of the nations concerning which the LORD said unto the children of Israel, Ye shall not go in to them, neither shall they come in unto you: for surely they will turn away your heart after their gods: Solomon clave unto these in love. And he had seven hundred wives, princesses, and three hundred concubines: and his wives turned away his heart.**

10. **Apostle Paul**- Said all these are mess, let me just serve God, he refused to get married just served God.

**First Corinthians 7: 32-35:**

**But I would have you without carefulness. He that is unmarried careth for the things that belong to the Lord, how he may please the Lord:**

**But he that is married careth for the things that are of the world, how he may please his wife.**

There is difference also between a wife and a virgin. The unmarried woman careth for the things of the Lord, that she may be holy both in body and in spirit: but she that is married careth for the things of the world, how she may please her husband.

And this I speak for your own profit; not that I may cast a snare upon you, but for that which is comely, and that ye may attend upon the Lord without distraction.

Many captured slaves and turned them into wives.

## NO PHYSICAL FORMULA PROVIDED FOR FINDING A WIFE, BUT THERE ARE SCRIPTURAL OR SPIRITUAL GUIDELINES.

The Bible does not give us a direct, exact, physical formula for finding a life partner unlike salvation, there is a way you know you are saved. I think because we are dealing with human beings.

**Genesis 2:21-25:**

And the LORD God caused a deep sleep to fall upon Adam, and he slept: and he took one of his ribs, and closed up the flesh instead thereof;

And the rib, which the LORD God had taken from man, made he a woman, and brought her unto the man.

And Adam said, This is now bone of my bones, and flesh of my flesh: she shall be called Woman, because she was taken out of Man

Therefore shall a man leave his father and his mother, and shall cleave unto his wife: and they shall be one flesh.

And they were both naked, the man and his wife, and were not ashamed.

The wife Adam married was made of the same substance, the same ideology, a woman taken out of him, the same composition, the same material, spiritual composition, biological composition.

Genesis 24 where Eliezer of Damascus, Abraham's eldest servant went to search for a wife for his Master's son Isaac, for now I will not go into that.

**There is no physical formula provided in the Bible for finding a life partner, but there are spiritual guidelines.**

1. **Proverbs 18:22: Whoso findeth a wife findeth a good thing, and obtaineth favour of the LORD.**

   Gives idea of searching, gives idea of desire.

   Automatically, man's responsibility is to find, search, desire, action will be required on your own part.

   Brothers, there is a finding, ladies you have to position yourselves.

2. **Amos 3:3: Can two walk together, except they be agreed?**

   **Amos 3:3** portrays the key to a successful marriage is not love. Can two walk together unless they agree? Agree means, compatibility, similarity, agreeableness: spiritual agreeableness, what is your ideology about God? What is your ideology about Ministry? If a man marries a lady because of beauty, what is her ideology about God? What is your ideology about culture? Ideological agreeableness, parenting agreeableness, financial agreeableness.

   Even if the person does not have the same ideology, is he/she teachable? Does he/she have the teachability? The person who has the same ideology.

   The Bible says, it is better to sit at the roof of your house, than to marry a contentious and angry lady. Do not spiritualise things. Brothers, take the lady to your church or where you have your spiritual food.

   **If there is no compatibility, there is no need to marry.**

3. **Proverbs 19:14: House and riches are the inheritance of fathers: and a prudent wife is from the LORD.**

   Meaning you can inherit houses and riches from your father and mother, but in marriage, you must involve God. A prudent wife/husband is from the Lord.

4. **Isaiah 30:21: And thine ears shall hear a word behind thee, saying, This is the way, walk ye in it, when ye turn to the right hand, and when ye turn to the left.**

Expect the leadership of the Holy Spirit in finding a life partner. My sheep hear my Voice.

5. **Luke 14:28:**

**"For which of you, intending to build a tower, sitteth not down first, and counteth the cost, whether he have sufficient to finish it?"**

This is a cost dimension of marriage. Which of you to be married will not count the cost? Start counting the cost. Am I ready to provide for my family? Am I ready to pay the children's school fees? Am I ready to die for my marriage? Am I ready to love her and protect her all the days of my life?

Am I ready to stay with her all the days of my life?

Am I ready to live with a woman all the days my life? Am I ready to love her?

## TWO PLACES IN THE SCRIPTURE THAT MARRIAGE CAME THROUGH VISION OR PROPHECY

1. **Prophet Hosea**, we saw God telling him to marry a prostitute.

**Hosea 1:1-3:**

**THE word of the LORD that came unto Hosea, the son of Be-e'ri in the days of Uz-ziàh, Jotham, Ahaz, and Hezekiah, kings of Judah, and in the days of Jer-o-boam the son of Jòash, king of Israel.**

**The beginning of the word of the LORD by Hosea. And the LORD said to Hosea, Go, take unto thee a wife of whoredoms and children of whoredoms: for the land hath committed great whoredom, departing from the LORD.**

**So he went and took Gòmer the daughter of Dib'la-im; which conceived, and bare him a son.**

2. **Joseph** being afraid that Mary was with a child.

According to Scripture, prophecy is not the way God reveals our life partners.

## THREE WAYS GOD SHOWS YOU WHOM TO MARRY

1. **Desire And Passion**- Not everybody is going to see a vision. Genuine passion, godly desire, I have seen this lady, I connect with her in spirit. Develop friendship.

2. **The Prophetic**- Either prophecy or the Ministry of the Holy Spirit in your life.

3. **Divne Connection**- Sister, in the house of God your husband is there. The Bible says, he that lives by the altar, eats by the altar. One of the strongest or greatest ways couples are connected together is serving in the house of God.

## TWO WAYS GOD USES VISION IN MARRIAGE

1. Based on your personal intimacy and yieldness to Him.

2. Nature and kind of your assignment, for instance, being in the ministry.

As a man of God/woman of God, God will not allow you to marry any type of person.

Prophecy can never be exalted above the Word.

Brother/Sister, the key to your marriage is in your hands.

Paul the Apostle was never married, still he said a lot of things about marriage.

Jesus was never married, but He said a lot of things about marriage.

## FOUR LEVELS OF MATURITY TO BE CONSIDERED BEFORE ENTERING INTO MARRIAGE

1. **Spiritual Maturity-1 Peter 2: 1-2: WHEREFORE laying aside all malice, and all guile, and hypocrisies, and envies, and all evil speakings, as newborn babes, desire the sincere milk of the word, that ye may grow thereby:**

You do not get born again now, and start looking for whom to marry. Grow in spirit, serve God as a single person, He will bless you with a good man. A good Christian marriage is salary paid by God. Be spiritually matured before going into marriage.

2. **Emotional Maturity**- A man is somebody people run to. You must be emotionally matured before going into marriage.

3. **Financial Maturity**- Particularly for the man. You need a job. If you still lives in your father's boys 'Quarters, do not get married. If your mother still pays your taxi fare to work, do not get married. **Psalm 3:3: But thou, O LORD, art a shield for me; my glory, and the lifter up of mine head.** Marriages fail because, financial is not settled. You need to be economically empowered especially for men. You must be financially empowered before you get married.

4. **Physical Maturity**- You must be physically matured.

## SOME WRONG REASONS PEOPLE GET MARRIED

1. **"I am too old"-** Do not marry because you are too old.

2. **Family Pressure**- Do not marry because of family pressure. I tell mothers to pray for their children and do not pressurize them.

Wait for God's time, God's time is the best.

3. **Peers' Pressure**- You want to marry because your mates are getting married.

# CHAPTER THREE

# How To Choose A Life Partner

The Biblical way of choosing a life partner is described in Genesis chapter two. God first created man and provided all his needs. After that, He presented him a wife. Now the Bible stated it clearly that a man looks for a wife, and when he finds a wife, there are ways of knowing that she is your wife, and if she is not your wife, you stay away from her (Proverbs 27:12). Proverbs 27:12 says, **A prudent man foreseeth the evil, and hideth himself; but the simple pass on, and are punished**. On the other hand, a woman is not supposed to go out searching for a husband. If a woman is in the Will of God, by serving and loving God, her husband will surely find her. A man needs to ask the Lord to show him his wife while he is in search for her. On the other hand, a woman must continue to serve God, and thank Him for the man He has created for her and rest assured that her husband will one day find her.

Both parties must pray in faith knowing that God will answer their prayers, but the man must be confident enough to speak to the woman for his acceptance.

There are some encouraging Scriptures: Matthew 7:7-8, Mark 10:27, Proverbs 27:12, Proverbs 18:20, Amos 3:3, Job 22:26-30.

## THE MAN: GENESIS 2:7-25

Before God created the woman, He first created the man and made sure He provided everything for the man, and gave him instructions on how to maintain them.

It is God's intention that before any man makes a decision to marry, he must have had some basic possessions, that is, self-sufficiency. It is very important that a man be self-sufficient before he marries: you do not have to be exceedingly rich, but at least enough to sustain you and your wife.

After God provided for Adam's needs, he said**, And the LORD God said, It is not good that the man should be alone; I will make him an help meet for him. (Genesis 2:18).** After God made the woman, He brought her to the man **(Genesis 2:22).** That means, it was God who provided a wife for Adam. It is the duty of every man to pray to God to provide his wife for him, just as He provided the woman for Adam. When God provided the woman for Adam, he took her with full acceptance and said they were one **(Genesis 2:23).**

## HOW DO YOU KNOW SHE IS FROM THE LORD?

**Proverbs 22:18:**

**For it is a pleasant thing if thou keep them within the; they shall withal be fitted in thy lips.**

**Proverbs 12:4:**

**A virtuous woman is a crown to her husband: but she that maketh ashamed is as rottenness in his bones.**

**Proverbs 19:14:**

**House and riches are the inheritance of fathers: and a prudent wife is from the LORD.**

When you find your wife, the favour of the Lord comes upon your life, you will not experience any stress, but joy and peace. She will always be willing to help you, and will want the best for you. She will not tear you down, or drain you financially, or self-centred, or egocentric, or narcissistic who will always want her own way. She will be ready "for better for worse".

The last quotation says, you can inherit riches and houses from your parents, but a prudent (wise, careful, sensible, far-sighted) wife can ONLY come from the Lord.

Now all these signs will not manifest in one day, but gradually as you continue to pray, God will let you run into your wife. These signs will come bit by bit.

But that does not mean when you get married, there will be no problem.

## THE WOMAN

One great aspect of Eve was that she was a worshipper, who acknowledged God for blessing her with children despite their sin in the garden. In actual fact, Eve was the first person to worship or acknowledge God.

Every woman has a seed of worship in her, and it is her duty to express it.

**Proverbs 31:10, 30, 31:**

**Who can find a virtuous woman? for her price is far above rubies?**

**Favour is deceitful, and beauty is vain: but a woman that feareth the LORD, she shall be prised.**

**Give her of the fruit of her hands; and let her own works praise her in the gates.**

Virtuous, means, good, righteous, honourable, upright, honest, these are characteristics you find in a woman who will make a wife.

**Both man and woman must be ready to live up to this Scripture below.**

This Scripture is presented in different Bible versions for better understanding.

**Colossians 3:18-19 (KJV):**

**18. Wives, submit yourselves unto your own husbands, as it is fit in the Lord.**

**19. Husbands, love your wives, and be not bitter against them.**

**Colossians 3:18-19 (Amplified Bible):**

**18. Wives, be subject to your husbands (subordinate and adapt yourselves to them), as is right and fitting and your proper duty in the Lord.**

**19. Husbands love your wives (be affectionate and sympathetic with them) and do not be harsh or bitter or resentful toward them.**

**Colossians 3: 18-19 (The Message Bible):**

**18: Wives understand and support your husbands by submitting to them in ways that honor the master.**

**19. Husbands, go all out in love for your wives. Do not take advantage of them.**

It is obvious from these Scriptures above, that each person has a role to play. Our God is not partial, both husband and wife have a role to play for the success of their marriage.

## CHOOSING THE RIGHT PARTNER

1. **You must be the right person.** You must be qualified to pick a wife.

2. **You must be spiritually compatible.** If you are a born again Christian, marry a fellow born again Christian. Some people are religious Christians, not born again. Somebody you can operate on the same spiritual wave-length, the same spiritual frequency. Somebody that has spiritual compatibility, not somebody that goes to church.

3. **Financial Capacity**- You must be financially equipped, especially the man.

   Real love involves material things.

4. **You must be strategic in meeting people**. You need to know the kind of places to meet a responsible person.

   A. Place of work.
   B. Church- Be involved in church, join departments, be around, walk around, be accessible, smile. Do not go to night club.

5. **Do not neglect the place of prayer.**

   You need to let God order your steps.

   **Psalm 37:23 says: The steps of a good man are ordered by the LORD: and he delighteth in his way**. Marry the person you are connected to. Marry your friend.

6. **Flow with Holy Spirit- Genesis 24:13-20**

   Not spiritual gifts, **but spiritual fruits as in Galatians 5: 22-23.**

## Roles of both in a nutshell

### The man

The husband is the head of the wife and the home. This is the constituted order which God Himself ordained. Here headship is not in the sense of being the "the boss of the show, the master's voice" in all matters, but in the sense of being a spiritual leader, directly in responsibility to God who is your head. The husband is to show deference to his wife as the weaker but not an inferior partner. She is her husband's equal in the grace or gift of life (1 Peter 3:7). The husband's role is to provide and protect the family: to give strength, support, stability and security. Unhappy is the home where authority and control are assumed by the wife because this is against God's injunction.

Many are the blessings when God's order is obeyed.

The man is the head that needs to be loving to his wife and not take advantage of his position and mistreat her. If a man can see his wife as a gift from God, and appreciate that gift by loving her as he loves himself, it will be very easy for him to play his role in the home.

Billy Sunday once said, "if you want your wife to be an angel, do not treat her like the devil."

### The woman

The wife is the heart of the home. She has a high and holy calling, and that is one of loving submission to her husband as the church submits to Christ. The apostle Paul declares, **Therefore as the church is subject unto Christ, so let the wives be unto their own husbands in everything (Ephesians 5:22- 24, Colossians 3:18, 1 Peter 3:1,2).**

"Was there ever a time when the true church felt that it did not want to be subject to Christ? Was there ever a time when Christ, the Head of the church, ruled and governed His flock like a ruthless tyrant? Has there ever been a time when you, as a Christian, has felt that Christ dealt with you in a loveless, unjust manner? Has there ever been a time when in obeying Christ you were made to feel like a dog obeying his master? Of course, the answer is no. The whole relationship is one of limitless love and not of tyranny and domination." O.W. Toelke.

A woman is a worshipper of God and therefore, she has a river of blessing that will flow out of her; that is why she stands as a gift to her husband. She must be submissive because of this river of blessings that will flow out of her, and not work in arrogance, or pride to her husband, because of the blessings in her. If a woman can present herself as the gift God has made her to be for her husband, it will be easy for her to play her role in the home.

In the words of AMC Claren, "No wife ever had a satisfactorily wedded life who did not look up to and reverence her husband."

The Word of God says, **... thy desire shall be to thy husband, and he shall rule over thee (Genesis 3:16b).**

In other words, she is to be helpful and responsive to every reasonable request of her husband.

## SEVEN (7) FACTORS TO CONSIDER BEFORE YOU MARRY ANYONE

Do not marry anybody just because you love the person, love is not enough reason to get married, only love cannot sustain marriage. There are other factors to consider. There are many people that got married only because of love but are now regretting that decision. They were blinded by love but marriage performed a miracle in their eyes, now they can clearly see their mistakes.

**What are these factors you need to consider before you marry?**

1. Love

   Because l said love is not enough reason to get married does not in any way negate the importance of love in marriage. It will take a book to explain the criticality of love in marriage.

   No marriage can survive without love. Anger, irritation, resentment, quarrels, frustrations etc., are inevitable when there is lack of love.

   To show you the importance of love, almost a whole chapter of the Bible is dedicated to that effect (See 1 Corinthians 13).

Love is one of the vital pillars that sustains a marriage but as we all know that one pillar does not sustain or hold a building, other pillars are needed.

So love is the first vital factor to consider.

Do you really love the person?

Does the person also love you?

2. Compatibility

Apart from love, another important factor to consider is compatibility.

Lack of compatibility is the leading cause of divorce around the world. Compatibility is defined as when two things are capable of existing together in harmony. For two people from different backgrounds, upbringing, culture, orientation, experience, education, philosophy and so on, to live peacefully and in harmony with each other, they must be compatible (See Luke 5:36-37).

These important areas you must be compatible with anyone you want to marry.

a. Spiritual Compatibility

   Do your spiritual beliefs and convictions align?

   Are both of you born again?

b. Purpose Compatibility

   Is there alignment in purpose? Are both of you walking towards the same direction?

c. Mental Compatibility

   Are both of you operating on the same frequency intellectually? Some people are analogue in thinking, while some are digital. Some are still operating with the mentality of the 7ᵗʰ century in the 21ˢᵗ century. When you hear, "This is not how my forefathers and ancestors did it," that is mentality speaking. Some men still believe a woman belongs to the kitchen and the other room.

d.  Health Compatibility

Does your genotype, blood group and Rhesus factor match?

What is your genotype status?

AS, SS, AA, AC, SC

What is your blood group?

A, B, O, AB.

What is your rhesus factor?

+ve or −ve?

e.  Personality Compatibility

According to research, a large percentage of what you do is influenced by your personality type.

What is your temperament?

Sanguine, Choleric, Melancholy, Phlegmatic.

Many couples are quarrelling and fighting today because they do not have this knowledge, they do not understand their partners. So, does your personality match?

f.  Sexual Compatibility

Are your sexual orientations, education, exposure align with the person?

What is your stand on oral sex, anal sex, BDS Mete?

What are the things you cannot do or accept when it comes to sex, do they align with your partner?

g.  Preference Compatibility

This talks about hobbies or things that interest one.

Is there an alignment?

See, when there is disparity in any of these areas of compatibility, it may result in conflicts in marriage.

Without compatibility, someone is definitely going to get hurt, either the couples or the children. Lack of health compatibility is the reason why we have many children today suffering from Sickle Cell disease.

I know a couple that have lost two (2) of their three (3) children because of this sickness. And these are children they spent almost twelve (12) years looking for.

Lack of health compatibility in Rh factor is one of the reasons why many women are having miscarriages.

3. The Will of God

The Will of God is another factor to consider before you marry anyone.

What is heaven saying about this person you are considering? What is God saying? The Will of God in marriage is simply the person whom God approves for you to marry. That is, some that God is pleased with and approves for you (See Matthew 3:17).

Now, this does not mean that God specially created one particular person for you to marry. There are some that God is pleased with and approves for you (See Matthew 3:17). There is nothing like that. But as a child of God, you need to carry God along in your choice of life partner.

4. Good Character

There are ladies that are in love with their guys that abuse them physically, emotionally, psychologically and otherwise, yet they will not leave them because of love.

These guys beat them blue and black, disrespect them, and do all manners of things to them, but they are still stuck with them. This is how many of them end up getting murdered in cold blood. The same applies to some guys. So, check for good character.

Because you love someone does not mean you will not check out his or her character. A person's character is who he or she is, and that is what you will live in marriage. When someone has a bad character, no matter how much you love the person, my dear you will suffer.

5.  Suitability

Water has levels. She gets sizes. Clothes have sizes, and so it is with marriage. Everybody is not your size. Even God understands this in Genesis 2:18, the Bible says, "The Lord God said, "It is not good for the man to be alone l will make a helper suitable for him." By explanation, suitability means when something is capable, qualified, fit, proper, and appropriate for something. You cannot put a squared peg in a round hole. Love notwithstanding, it is not everyone that is suitable for you, your personality, your purpose, convictions, aspirations etc. Look for your size. Find your levels.

6.  Agreement

The Bible asks this important question in Amos 3:3, "Do two walk together unless they have agreed to do so? The answer is a capital No!

By definition, agreement is the state of being of one opinion about something or harmony of opinion, action, or character.

There are issues that a couple need to be in agreement if they will navigate the ocean of marriage successfully.

Take for an instant, a feminist and a non- feminist, these two people are different in opinion when it comes to submission, order and leadership in marriage.

If they are not in agreement in this area, what do you think will happen? I leave the answer to you.

As a man, you want to marry a housewife, a woman that will stay at home and take care of the home and the children, yet you will not look for such a woman to marry. You will be looking for an ambitious career driven woman and want to force her to stay at home, you are looking for trouble, Sir! Lack of agreement will lead to conflicts, irreconcilable differences and if these are not managed properly, the continuity of the marriage will be under threat.

7. Yokability

In 2 Corinthians 6:14, the Bible says, **Do not be yoked together with unbelievers. For what do righteousness and wickedness have in common? Or what fellowship can light have with darkness.**

In Israel, the farmers have a practice of yoking two animals of the same kind, say two donkeys, together for the purpose to plough the ground for plantation. The two animals that are yoked must be of the same kind. You cannot yoke a donkey and a sheep together, you cannot yoke a donkey and a cow together. That is an unequal yoke.

Marriage is a yoke. It yokes two people of the same kind and with the same purpose together.

A believer and unbeliever are unequal yoke, because, both of them are different. They carry different natures and have different purposes. Because of love, many zealous sisters got married to unbelieving partners, today they are nowhere to be found in the faith. Their husbands stopped them from going to church and rubbished their Christian lives.

The same applies to some brothers. When you yoke a donkey with a sheep together, there will be a problem. The donkey is likely to strangulate the sheep to death or the donkey may end up having a hunchback as a result of bending. So, ask yourself, can l be yoked with this person and there will not be any problem?

If you do not want to be strangulated to death or develop a hunchback, my dear look for your mate. Your progress in life will either be accelerated or decelerated, it all depends on who you marry. So, these are the factors you need to consider before you venture into marriage. No matter how much you love someone, if these factors are not checked, l bet you, there will be problems. Make your marital journey as easy as possible by getting it rightly from the beginning.

This is the reason why we have prayer, friendship, dating and courtship. They are not for frivolities. They are agencies and mercenaries for getting things rightly.

I hope you can see now, that love is not enough reason to get married to someone.

# QUALITIES OF A MAN TO MARRY

## FOUR THINGS A MAN SHOULD HAVE BEFORE YOU MARRY HIM THERE ARE CERTAIN THINGS A LADY MUST FIND IN A MAN OTHERWISE DO NOT MARRY HIM.

I have summarized every sister's cry just to four things. Any brother who does not come along these lines is dangerous. I did not say he is bad, l say he is dangerous. I do not care whether the brother has a Bible on top of his head, if these four are not in place, your home will be in disaster.

1. **God-Fearing**

   **Maximum Husband and Father**

   You have no business talking about relationship and marriage with any man who is not GOD-FEARING.

   **(Proverbs 22:17; Hebrews 10:24; Psalm 128:1-4)** Psalm shows that to be God´s kind of husband and father, you must be a man that fears God. Appropriate fear of God makes a man an unusual blessing to his wife and children. The fear of God will be the soil out of which the man's positive influence will grow and the basic reason a man's family will arise and call him blessed.

   Do not be too fast, allow me to define what l mean by God-fearing. Notice l do not say born again, because, that thing has been abused in the 21st century.

   A born again brother is not one who came out for altar call and you witnessed him raising his hand.

   To be God-fearing, the primary reason society is in decadence, listen to me, is, because, the men are not God-fearing. The fear of the Lord is not believing in God, they are two different things. I can have faith in God, and not fear God. Faith in God and fear of God are not the same. There are many faith-filled Christians who are not God-fearing. Look at this, I am a Christian, l am a child of God. My life is governed by a reference.

   Listen, the Bible is my reference. My decisions are made with respect to this reference. So, when you tell me you are a husband, what reference are you leading your life and your family?

What does it mean to be God-fearing?

To be God-fearing number one means:

a. To have reference, respect for God. Not just to believe in God, but to have reference for Him.

b. Number two, to be God-fearing, means, to submit to the ways of God. Submit to the Word of God as the final authority in all matters, not some matters. There is nothing like a man who submits to the Will of God in all matters. So, you do not mix the Word of God and culture. Men are not bad people, but there are concepts which have turned men into pieces. There is no family that will suffer if he follows the Will of God. The configuration of a man is that they have a lot to protect. Intrinsically, the configuration of a man shows masculinity. I am an ardent follower of the Word. Completely anti-Christ in approach. He does not have to be a Pastor, has nothing to do with a Pastor, or prayer warrior. There is nothing like a young man who submits to the Will of God. It is being God-fearing that will not make you raise your hands upon your wife. The Bible says, Husbands love your wives as Christ loved the church. While we were still sinners, Christ died for us. We were not even qualified. There are some cultures that say to beat their wives. An ardent follower of the Word, not what you like, but what the Word of God said. Even if I do not like the Word of God, I will still remain there. Refusal to conform to the Word of God has brought problems in families. Train and mentor your children. The Bible says, train a child the way he should go, when he is old will not depart from it (Proverbs 22:6).

## 2. Submission To An Earthly Authority

The second in this order, must be in this order. The second thing is that, the man must submit to an earthly authority.

Must submit to an earthly authority for mentorship, for building, for correction.

There are many families in trouble today, because, there is no authority figure over the life of the husband.

There is no man that can call him, and say what he is doing is wrong.

He can beat the wife and almost kill her. He is a god of himself.

There must be an authority he submits. Sisters, please hear me in the name of Jesus, twenty-first century, things have changed.

Never marry a man who does not have a Pastor, a mentor, spiritual authority, or an elderly person, someone he could listen to. There must be a personality that he has covenanted to listen to. The man must be able to show who his authority is. The Bible says, let everything be done decently and orderly. Ruth told Naomi, your God will be my God, your people will be my people.

Listen, no matter how wrong a man and a woman are, if there is someone for them to listen to, you are still save.

3. **Must Have Love/ Passion For You**

If you are married and your husband does not have this, begin to labour in the place of prayer. Lord, turn the heart of this man, he must be God-fearing. I have married, the deed has been done, but Lord, you can still step in. You are the God of second chance.

Number three, sister, you are praying or considering a man to marry, or you are married, THAT MAN MUST HAVE PASSION FOR YOU, not love.

Passion is an adjective that qualifies the extent of love. I love you is not a language that is useful again this generation, because, it has been abused. Any man who does not have passion for you will be unfaithful. Passion is more than physical attraction. Any marriage where there is no passion, there must be unfaithfulness. Passion is the dept of love that you are contented. There is an appetite for discontentment in the body of Christ. A man who will love his wife and respect her.

**Ephesians 5:21, 25:**

**Submitting yourselves one to another in the fear of God.**

**Husbands, love your wives, even as Christ also loved the church, and gave himself for it;**

**Four Types Of Men If You Marry That Are Exposed To People:**

**A**. Man of God

B. High Level Business Man

C. Politicians

D. Lecturer

Because they see all kinds of women. If you are married, pray for passion for your husband.

4. **Never Marry A Man Who Is Irresponsible**

**First Timothy 5:8: But if any provide not for his own, and specially for those of his own house, he hath denied the faith, and is worse than an infidel.**

**Measure of responsibility**

**What does it mean to be responsible?**

To be responsible means to be aware of cost dimension of life- taking cognizant of the cost dimension of life. Responsibility is a burden of obligation over someone or something. Responsibility is an awareness of consequence that if you do this, there is a consequence, and if you do not do this, there is a consequence. I do not mean money, anything that is to be done must be done by someone. Is irresponsibility that produces laziness. Many young men have been over-pampered. There are people whose wives are suffering, cannot pay their children's School fees. Average African family is to take care of nuclear family. Brothers, is better to end a relationship than to have a scattered marriage. Responsibility is not having a car, or house. Responsibility is the willingness to press cost dimension of life.

# QUALITIES OF A WOMAN TO MARRY

## FIVE THINGS A WOMAN SHOULD HAVE BEFORE YOU MARRY HER-WHAT KIND OF WOMAN SHOULD YOU MARRY?

1. **God-fearing**- gender irrespective, the same as the man.

Women who are not God-fearing will have their husbands and sponsors.

Sponsor for remedies, husband for every other thing. That is why they do not bother to change their husbands. Some married women who are not God-fearing still have affiliations with their former boy friends, still call their ex- boyfriends even in their marriage. That is why they are not faithful, not desperate to change their husbands.

2. **Submissiveness** –Submit to the man at all times.

**Ephesians 5:21-24:**

**Submitting yourselves one to another in the fear of God.**

**Wives, submit yourselves unto your own husbands, as unto the Lord.**

**For the husband is the head of the wife, even as Christ is the head of the church: and he is the saviour of the body.**

**Therefore as the church is subject unto Christ, so let the wives be to their own husbands in everything.**

Submission is not a choice, is mandatory. Submission is a risk, you do not know the man very well. When you marry, you discover other things. Is a risk, needs Holy Spirit. That is why the authority you submit must be vetted by God. Idea that the man must be capable before submission, you are a hypocrite. Submission starts from the relationship. If you are playing your role well, if the man is not doing well, that authority will come in.

3. **Sacrificial and Hospitable**

There are many ladies who cannot sacrifice for the growth of their homes. There are ladies who cannot inconvenience themselves for the sake of the family. There are some women when their husbands lose jobs, their attitudes change, will not respect the man again. Never submit to a man because he has money. If you want to do it God's way, you must submit, there is no room for rebellion. There are some women who sit with their friends and lambast their husbands. Some ladies expose their husbands to their friends, discuss family affairs, reveal family secrets. How do you expect those people to respect your husband again? There are ladies who are not hospitable, stingy attitudes. The Bible tells every woman to cover her head. There is physical and spiritual covering. There are women who have stingy attitudes. You must learn to sacrifice. There are many homes once the man does not have money you see the body language. There are many brothers who are suffering in the hands of ladies.

4. **Physical Attractiveness-** Must be physically attractive. Beauty is a relative statement. Physical is important, but it will fade like a leaf. If the only reason why you are attracted to a woman is physical factor, when the physical factor supersedes fear of God, supersedes submission, supersedes sacrificial and hospitable, you are in trouble. Spiritualise your process of getting a wife. Do not be carnal.

Do not carry a lady you will not be proud of. Ladies, look physically attractive. Brothers, if you want that of a glamorous lady, start working on yourself as soon as possible. You must be physically attractive, both parties, be smart. If you are looking for a man who is perfect, you do not have ministry in that man. Your duty is to complement the man.

5. **Responsibility (1 Timothy 5:8)**

Responsibility is a burden of obligation over someone or something. Responsibility is an awareness of consequence if you do this, there is a consequence, if you do not do, there is a consequence.

## REASONS WHY PEOPLE ARE NOT RESPONSIBLE

1. Indecision over their successes and establishment.

2. Admit your mistakes

3. Stop blaming other people for your problems.

**Proverbs 21:20: There is treasure to be desired and oil in the dwelling of the wise; but a foolish man spendeth it up.**

For brothers, spirit of a waster; wasted opportunities, resources, spirit of waste.

You cannot reap a seed you have not sowed. You cannot sow a seed of wickedness and reap a good man.

# CHAPTER FOUR

# Whom Should I Marry?

A. **Must Be In Christ**- There are standards for every Christian relationship. Does this relationship worship God? If this relationship reduces divinity, reduces God, is not worth going into it (Romans 12:1-2). Does not make you **reduce your Christianity, reduce your spirituality. If you are born again**, marry a fellow born again. Do not be unequally yoked. Do not be married to unbeliever. Somebody who is not born again is dead. Someone whose heart is worshipping God. God created marriage. God said in Malachi that the reason He created marriage is to have godly seeds. You cannot marry someone who is not in the same spiritual frequency or spiritual wavelength with you. **Must be in Christ.**

B. **Character-** Check the character. How does he/she behave when he is not in church?

C. **Companionship-** Marry your friend. **Companionship is the major thing marriage is made up of**. Pick one of your friends. Start as a friend. You spend time talking to your spouse, not only sex. Some marriages, they are not friends, no conversation, no companionship. Can you talk? Sex is not intimacy. If you are having sex before marriage, before you get there you are already tired.

D. **Readiness.** You must be ready.

E. **Define the relationship.** Which type of relationship? When do you want to marry?

# THREE DIMENSIONS A MAN MUST FOUND HIMSELF BEFORE MARRIAGE

There has been confusion in area of marriage. At what age will you marry? Is it when you graduate? For any man graduating, advancement in age is not enough to marry. Some provisions in the Bible are to make us know you are ready for marriage. God operates in multifaceted dimensions. You see God as Rapha, Sabaoth, Jireh, Elohim, and so on.

The same applies to man. Watch this: Men are not husbands. Many Pastors are poor husbands. There are many Pastors, celebrities who are starving their wives for these dimensions.

1. **As a husband-** Defines the scope of his ministry to his wife. Defines his intimacy to his wife, her emotional needs, her financial needs. Gives his wife emotional security. Protects the wife emotionally. Ministry to your wife, intimacy with your wife- meeting her emotional needs.

2. **As a father-** You are not a father when you have children. Father is a Greek word **"Abba"**- means source and sustainer, when you are the originator of a thing. Father is when you are a provider and a protector.

   First Timothy 5:8: Any man who cannot provide/protect the family is worst than an infidel. Provide- love, food, shelter, security, spiritual guidance. Protect your family from physical hazards, emotional security. You are a father according to your ability to provide. If you want to marry, are you a father? Ability to provide- food, love, mentorship, protect your family from physical hazards. You are not a father by age, by spiritual, or physical. Is your ability to provide. Fatherhood is ability to provide and protect. You neglect fatherhood when you ignore your responsibilities. Brother say, in the name of God, I receive grace to provide for my family and protect my family. Father is a sense of responsibility. Many men, people have produced babies, but they are not a father You are a father, because, you provide for your family. It starts from relationships.

3. **Priest/Spiritual Head of the home-** According to God's organ for family, the woman and the children should look up to the man for guidance. The man is the Priest, the Spiritual head of the home. Every man is instituted by God to be a Priest, or the spiritual head of the family. Every man must take a position. Ladies, that is why it matters to marry someone who knows God. According to God's

organ for marriage or family, is the man that should be the spiritual head, the Priest of the family. The man should teach the children, teach the family about God, lead in Bible studies, prayers, priestly responsibility, spiritual head. It starts from relationships. For example, your wife is pregnant, you lay hand on her stomach and pray for her. Your son brings a result you see is not motivating, you lay hands on your son, pray and declare, every son should be like the father. Is very important, that is why you have to marry a man who knows God. It may not be easy for the ladies, because, they have to submit. If the lady is more spiritual, as a man, are you ready to catch up? A man with capacity in spirit. Brothers, when you become a husband, father and Priest/ Spiritual Head, then, you are ready for marriage.

## THREE DIMENSIONS A LADY MUST FOUND HERSELF BEFORE MARRIAGE

**There are three (3) dimensions to every woman and you must not fail in any of them.**

The first is the Heart of a Wife, the second is the Heart of a Mother, and the third is the Heart of a Minister/Priesthood. If you fail in any of these dimensions, then you have failed in your destiny.

1. **As a wife**- Ministry of a wife is to your husband alone, do not bring uncles. Defines the entire scope of your ministry to your husband. You bring the king out of the man by meeting his emotional needs, and by being physically attractive for him. I am not talking about nudity and seduction. A lady is created to make a man feel like a man. It matters, and it starts from relationships. Every brother, there is a king, bring the king out of him. When was last you made the man feel like a king? Vatshi stopped being a wife, she was sent out of the palace. Esther/Hadassah prepared a banquet, and the king said, why prepared the banquet? Esther said, just to herald your kingdom. The king asked her," what do you want?" She said to give her half of the kingdom. Initially, when you married him, you used to bring food for him in a tray and respect him, but now you carry the juice in your hand as if you are selling juice. Ladies, lock your husband's attention to you.

Ladies say, in the name of Jesus, I receive the grace to be a wife in deed. There is a difference between secular relationship and Christian or godly relationship. Have you brought joy to your husband? Since you married your husband, have you brought him favour? Since you came his ego went down, finances went down.

He that finds a wife, finds something good and obtains favour from the Lord.

There are many women, but few wives. A man can build the house, a wife builds a home and creates a conducive atmosphere.

2. **Mother (Home maker)**- There is the Heart of a mother which defines the jurisdiction of your ministry to your children, both spiritually, physically and the people that God will connect you with. Key word under mother is sacrifice. A man can build a house, but it takes a woman to make a home, conducive atmosphere. Meeting your husband's emotional needs, looking physically attractive for your husband. Your physical attraction to your husband matters a lot, and it starts from relationships. Make your husband feel like a king. Bring out a king from your husband. Mother is the maker of home.

3. **Minister/Priesthood** – The Heart of a Minister defines the scope of your assignment and that which you have been sent to do. You can be an effective minister and a bad wife. Every woman must be on her knees, create an altar especially if you are married to a man of God. An altar is a place where humanity enters into covenant with divinity. Ladies can discern in spirit more than men. Intercede for your husband, your family. Men can be egoistic. There is a priestly dimension to a woman. Beauty without God is nonsense, added to that beauty, is spirituality.

The Bible says in Proverbs 18:22, whoso findeth a wife findeth a good thing, and obtaineth favour of the LORD. He did not say, finding the woman makes her a wife, you must be a wife first to be found. The word wife, is a quality and not a personality, it is not marriage that makes a woman a wife, he that finds a woman who is already a wife, has found a good thing. Many men found women, but they did not find good things, can l talk to you please? The average ladies' concept of relationship right now is that l am beautiful, and a young man will just come and carry me, keeps spending money on me, buy things for me, you know where we learnt it our Nigerian films.

I do not insult our entertainment industry, but that is it, they show it there, the guy is always kneeling down, crawling, and running to the lady, and her concept of marriage is entering rest and joy.

There are many of us right now, the concept that we have about marriage is very troubling and disturbing. It is very interesting, God needs to help us, hallelujah. Anything you are not taught, you will not excel. Many people guess how motherhood should be, but l want to challenge all the ladies here, make quality investments in your life, there are tapes and books, to listen and read. Brothers, do not let the beauty of a lady fool you.

Sisters say after me, in the name of Jesus, l am a woman of excellence, in the name of Jesus, l am a woman of virtue, l am a woman of grace, l am a woman of power, l am a blessing to my husband, to my children, they will call me blessed for the hand of the Lord is upon me, Amen.

## THREE THINGS THAT TELL YOU WHETHER YOU ARE A MOTHER OR NOT

A. **Kitchen**- Kitchen is where meals are made, health is made. Your kitchen is a reflection of your motherhood ability. There are many people their kitchens are a mess. Sink is dirty, the trash pan is filled with dirt not thrown away. Proverbs 31 refers to a virtuous woman. Your kitchen has to be clean always. Mother, a home maker. Are you a mother? Many ladies are not mothers. You can be a mother if you make your decision.

B. **Your Toilet**-In many homes, their toilets are a disaster. One universal towel for everybody including visitors. One universal sponge. Toilet is not flushed, is dirty. The children running out of house with mucous and dirty. The bucket is worn out. You do not expect the man to start going to buy a new bucket. How many ladies are proactive? All kinds of domestic things you want the man to do, that is the work of a mother. There are things a woman is supposed to do. If a man does it, he is doing it out of his way.

C. **Your Living Room (Parlour)**-Everything is scattered, everything is unkempt, everything is in a state of disarray, or chaotic situation. Papers on the floor, dust everywhere, children running out with mucous. The key word under motherhood is sacrifice. If there is no heart of sacrifice, you are not a mother. Have you seen a mother do an honour and give the credit to the husband? How many of you can do good and give credit to the husband? You dress the husband and give credit to him. Must receive grace to be mother. A mother does not have glory for herself, her pride is her husband and children.

These three places have to be clean always. A good mother will sacrifice.

## A HAPPY HOME NEEDS A GOOD WOMAN

A good woman makes a happy home, all things being equal. God gave the woman the assignment of home-making. In **Proverbs 14:1, the word says, EVERY wise woman buildeth her house: but the foolish pluketh it down with her hands.**

She is a teacher- the first teacher of every child.

She is the friend- the first friend of every child.

She is her husband's wife- mother, and friend. In the woman is rolled the quality of succour, love, care, nurture, and warmth.

A man calls his wife, his friend and mother. A suitor, should have open eyes. **Do you see any of these qualities?**

A woman without compassion is dangerous. A woman overly selfish is dangerous. **The home needs a woman complete with her kit of home making qualities.**

When you- a man is only looking at her legs, face, - admiring her beauty, you do forgot the important inner qualities. It is these qualities that give her the leadership in management of the home. The man is the head, the provider- the woman is the resource manager, the home manager and the hand that not only rocks cradle, but "strokes" everyone.

A woman should be by nature selfless, hard working and nurturant. Check those qualities out. **Above all, a woman should be very close to God, and even if her husband is not a worshipper of God, she should take the family to the Lord and cover all of her own with her prayers.**

A woman should see herself as God does- His partner in procreation, nurture and redemption; and behave accordingly- especially be the CONSCIENCE of the family. **A man should watch out for a good woman for a good home.**

## THE VIRTUOUS WOMAN

The virtuous woman earned her good marks in exemplary good behaviour.

A virtuous woman scores and is rated highly from the home by her children, husband, outsiders, and by God.

She is praised for looking well to the affairs and ways of her household as an excellent home maker, and home manager, full of wisdom.

**Proverbs 14:1 says, Every wise woman buildeth her house (home); but the foolish woman plucketh it down with her hands.**

A key principle is for women to agree with God that it is part of a woman's wisdom to treasure her home; and to invest all in her to build it without any stint.

## QUALITIES OF THE VIRTUOUS WOMAN PROVERBS 31:10-31

The virtuous woman earned her good marks in personal good qualities.

She is:

Reliable

Her husband trusts her.

She is industrious and brings in food from her hard work.

Feeds her household regularly. This means that she can spend her own money to augment whatever food money her husband is giving her.

Is good with her hands, makes and sells things.

Gives to the poor.

Invests for the future in savings.

Sews clothing for the family.

Opens her mouth with wisdom, discretion, kindness, gentleness, and no yelling.

Is a home manager and looks well to the ways of her household.

Her children call her **blessed.**

Her **husband commends** her.

# HOW DO I ATTRACT A GUY?

A. Be kind to everybody. Rebecca was kind to the servant of Abraham, Eliezer of Damascus.

B. Ruth was kind to her mother-in-law Naomi.

C. Moses was kind to Reuel's seven daughters that came to draw water.

Moses defended the seven daughters of Reuel (Jethro) against marauding shepherds (Exodus 2:16, 17).

## SEVEN BIBLICAL REQUIREMENTS FOR YOUR MARRIAGE TO WORK

1. Forgive and forget the past.

2. Husband is the spiritual head of the family, provider, and the prophet.

3. The wife has to be submissive **(Ephesians 5:22-24).**

4. **Ephesians 6:2-3:**

   **Honour thy father and mother; which is the first commandment with promise;**

   **That it may be well with thee, and thou mayest live long on the earth.**

   **Exodus 20:12: Honour thy father and thy mother: that thy days may be long upon the land which the LORD thy God giveth thee.**

   Children obey your parents, blessing with condition, so that your days will be long on earth.

5. Not good for a man to be alone, that is, communication. When communication stops flowing in your marriage, your marriage dies.

6. **Sexuality**

   Sex is meant to be a blessing.

God created sex as good.

a.  To express the oneness of the marriage covenant (Genesis 2:24, 4:1).

b.  To produce children (Genesis 4:1).

c.  For the mutual enjoyment of husband and wife (Prov.5:18, Deut. 24:5, Heb. 13:4, Song of Solomon 1:2, 13-16, 7:1-10, 4:1-7, 5:10-16).

**First Corinthians 7:4: The wife hath not power of her own body, but the husband: and likewise also the husband hath not power of his own body, but the wife.**

Your body is not your own. Stop manipulating yourselves. What will keep your marriage is back to back sex. The moment you marry, your body is his, and his body is yours. You have to give him sex whenever he needs it.

7.  **Husband and Wife**- Husband love your wife as Christ loved the church **(Ephesians 5:25).** Wives reverence your husbands. The choice is yours. Rationalization of your behaviour.

## THE BASIC THINGS A HUSBAND NEEDS FROM THE WIFE

1.  **Submissiveness- Ephesians 5:22-24: Wives, submit yourselves unto your own husbands, as unto the Lord.**

    **For the husband is the head of the wife, even as Christ is the head of the church: and he is the saviour of the body.**

    **Therefore as the church is subject unto Christ, so let the wives be to their own husbands in everything.**

    **Proverbs 15:32-33: He that refuseth instruction despiseth his own soul: but he that heareth reproof getteth understanding.**

    **The fear of the LORD is the instruction of wisdom; and before honour is humility.**

    A wise woman submits to her husband. Allow your husband to be decision- maker and leader of your house. When you submit to your husband, you submit to the

Lord. Eve did not submit to Adam, that was why she listened to the serpent. Sarah called Abraham my lord.

**Titus 2:3-5: The aged women likewise, that they be in behaviour as becometh holiness, not false accusers, not given to much wine, teachers of good things.**

**That they may teach the young women to be sober, to love their husbands, to love their children.**

**To be discreet, chaste, keepers at home, good, obedient to their own husbands, that the word of God be not blasphemed.**

The wife should reverence and honour the husband.

2. **Caring/ Serving - Proverbs 31:14-15: She is like the merchants' ships; she bringeth her food from afar.**

**She riseth also while it is yet night, and giveth meat to her household, and a portion to her maidens.**

The wife should be caring, providing good food for the husband, and rendering him good service. Every husband needs special care and treatment from the wife. Serve him, believe in him, stand by him. Do not be a Jezebel in the house, or a Jezebel in the church. You are so proud, you are so cocky. Support your husband.

The wife should also be prudent, not extravagant, a good home manager that manages the home well.

3. **A Wise Woman Takes Care Of Herself** – Every man wants a woman who is very neat. Your kitchen, living room, toilet and even your physical appearance.

Whatever your husband wants, wear it for him. Try to please him. Look nicely.

You are permitted to tempt your husband.

You have to have inward clothes and outside clothes. Inward clothes are for your husband, while outside clothes are for outing. Dress well, look smartly, keep yourself clean and attractive for your husband. Even the way you make the bed in the bedroom can attract your husband. You could put nice perfume in the bed, the pillow and under the pillow, you put sexy night gown for your husband, even nice perfume in your hair attracts your husband, shave your armpit, leave it clean, put nice deodorant in your armpit, and good perfume in your body. You should smell good always; no body odour, or dirty and bushy armpits, or mouth odour, dirty or scattered hair, or finger nails. Men are hunters.

Look good, dress well, be very presentable, and it shall be well with you in the name of Jesus.

The house should be clean always and orderly.

**First Corinthians 14:40: Let all things be done decently and in order.**

Some women when they marry, they will no longer take care of themselves, feeling after all they are married. Do not leave yourself uncared for because you are now married.

4. **Wisdom Of Speech-** The wife should be wise in choosing the right words and the right time for conversation.

**Proverbs 15:23: A man hath joy by the answer of his mouth: and a word spoken in due season, how good is it!**

Do not bring complaints to your husband immediately he comes back from work, or when he is eating. Do not nag, harass, or abuse your husband, you should respect your husband always.

5. **Coitus- Sexual Need – Genesis 2:25; 1 Corinthians 7:3-5**

The wife should satisfy the husband's sexual needs.

Never manipulate your husband with sex, or refuse him sex because he did not grant your request. **1 Corinthians 7:4-5.**

Do not use sex as a means of vengeance for your husband. Never use sex for an exchange of gift. For example, "except you give me this or that l will not allow you to have me". Give your husband a satisfactory and quality sex, and make him to feel like a man. Give sex to your husband duly not sparingly. That is the husband's conjugal right. It has been proved that when a man does not ejaculate, it can lead to prostrate cancer, anger, unnecessary masturbation. Use good sex to keep your husband warm and close to you constantly. **Song of Solomon 4:9-11.**

Prepare yourself, your mind, and the bed waiting to give your husband a wonderful sex surprise. **Proverbs 7:16–18.**

Sex is not only for having children; it is also for pleasure. You can enjoy sex with your husband. **Song of Solomon 8:6–7.**

Women who wear three pants at a time and tight knickers preventing their husbands from touching them are simply giving room for the devil to destroy their marriages. **1 Corinthians 7:5.** Quality sex is a way of building your home. **Ecclesiastes 9:9.**

What will keep your marriage is back to back sex. The moment you marry, your body is his, and his body is yours. You have to give him sex whenever he needs it.

Seduce your husband. You can invite your husband to have sex with you, is your husband.

6. **A Wise Woman Will Boost Her Husband's Ego**

A man wants a woman who will boost his ego, make him feel important.

Never insult your husband especially in the presence of people. A home is:

a. Father's kingdom

b. Mother's mission field

c. Children's paradise.

Your husband is a king in that kingdom, that is his kingdom. Respect him, honour him, boost his ego. If he is a preacher, when he is preaching, hail him, boost his ego. Speak to him with ego, speak to him with respect. When your husband enters applaud him.

Let his plate be different, let his cup be different and his cutlery different, is a king in that kingdom. Some people when visitors come, they bring out the best plates, everything and serve them, after they pack them back. Believe in him, celebrate him. Even if you earn more than him, or older than him, it does not matter, respect him.

Let people know you value what you have. Write notes to your husband, let him know you believe in him.

# ELEVEN (11) ROLES OF A HUSBAND TO HER WIFE

There are certain roles which wives play in the lives of their husbands which are not known to most men.

Check these out one after the other so as to appreciate your wife.

1. Lover: Your wife is a lover; not just a wife, express your love to her. Love her with all your heart, let anybody that cares to listen know.

2. Friend: Your wife is your friend, confide in her, nurture her, rejoice with her, mourn with her, celebrate her, and mostly, laugh with her.

3. Baby: Treat her like a baby. Pamper her, carry her, nurture her, nourish her, cherish her and feed her. Let her sleep in your bosom, cuddle her and let her feel comfortable with you.

4. Room Mate: Stay in the same room with her, what God has joined together, let no room put asunder.

5. Bed Mate: Do not just stay in the same room with her, sleep in the same bed, make her your bed mate.

6. Soul Mate: Your wife is not just a friend, she is your soul mate. Do not just join your hand with her, give her your mind, do not hide anything from her. Rejoice with this beautiful queen that is your wife.

7. Sex Partner: Your wife is your sex partner, do not be ashamed of making love with her. Stripe yourself naked, enjoy yourself, make sure she enjoys it too. Do not be selfish, look at her face, and check whether she enjoys it. Never go to bed with any other lady, it is a sin.

8. Your Queen: Treat your wife like a queen which she is; if you do, she will treat you as a king. If you are a king, treat her with respect, talk to her with honour, let marriage be honourable.

9. Your First Lady: Your wife should be your first lady, the number one woman in your life. Never allow any other woman, your mother, sisters, Secretary or colleagues take her position in your life.

10. Mother: Let your wife be like a mother to you. Confide in her.

11. Your Student: Teach your wife what you want her to do. Do not be annoyed with her; let her keep on learning from you, you are her number one teacher.

Treat your wife well so that your blessings will not be impeded or hindered.

When you have problem with your wife, your prayer can be hindered. Do not allow outsiders to know what is happening in your home. Settle your problems within yourselves, do not invite third party or outsiders to settle your problems, it will exacerbate or aggravate the whole thing.

Say sorry when you are wrong. Do not leave issues unattended, attend to them immediately. If issues accumulate, they will escalate. Another thing as regards to misunderstanding is patience, forgiving each other.

You will not fail in marriage in Jesus' name.

## TWENTY- THREE (23) THINGS TO DO TO KEEP YOUR HUSBAND UNDER THE CONTROL OF YOUR LOVE

1. Call him by a pet name, not Daddy Joseph, you are a bush girl.

   Names like, Darling, Sweetie, Honey, Baby, Sweetheart, Precious and so on.

2. Allow him exercise his authority as the head of the family.

3. Do not challenge him when he is hurt.

4. Be silent when he is angry.

   You can go back to him in his sober moment with apology and explain why you behaved that way that annoyed him.

5. Be quick to say, "1 am sorry dear," when ever you offend him, insist on his forgiveness, appreciate and kiss him when he does.

6. Speak good of him before his friends and siblings.

7. Honour his mother.

8. Insist that he buys gift for his parents and so be sure that he will do same for your parents.

9. Surprise him with his favourite dish especially when he does not have enough money at hand, and never delay his food.

10. Do not allow the maid to serve him food when you are at home, because you may lose him to them.

11. Give him a warm reception with an embrace when he returns, collect his luggage and help undress him.

12. Smile when you look at him and give him occasional pecks when you are out socially.

13. Praise him before your children sometimes.

14. Wash his back while he is in the tub or shower.

15. Put love note in his lunch box or briefcase.

16. Phone and tell him that you miss him.

17. Dial his number and on hearing "hello" just tell him, "1 love you."

18. If he is a public figure or politician, gently wake him at the early hours of the morning and romance him to the point of demand. He will not be enticed by any other woman that day. When you have satisfied your husband sexually, his emotion will be stable.

19. Tell him how lucky you are to have him as your husband.

20. Appreciate God for the Adam of your life.

21. Give him a hug for no reason.

22. Always remember to pray for him.

23. Pray together, and also pray together before going to bed in the evening.

May God bless Your Marriages. Singles, may you experience true love today and forever.

May non- serious people that waste your life be disconnected in your life in Jesus' name.

REMAIN EVER BLESSED!!!

## AS A WOMAN, YOU ARE MANY THINGS TO YOUR HUSBAND

As a woman, you are many things to your husband. Do not marry a man because of what he drives, but what drives him. Seduce your husband.

Do not always allow your husband to ask for sex. You can invite your husband to have sex with you, is your husband.

As a woman your under wear should match. You must be a different woman to your husband every time. Be creative. Do not be predictable. Give him what he wants. Every woman has an influence. If you lose influence over your husband, you have lost womanhood. You must learn to synchronize with your husband, blend with him.

Show interests in his interests. Be virtuous woman. Take care of him.

Be part of his plans. Do not have too many children. Sex is not all about making children. Dress to please your husband. Do fix time to have sex with your husband. When a man is sexually satisfied, he is emotionally stable. As a woman, you should invest in yourself spiritually so you can adequately support him. Build yourself as a prayer warrior so that you will not be forced to pray at the end of your life.

As a woman, you are a helper! The one you are helping must be stronger than you! Once you are married, you are somebody's helper, and the helper is meant to have what the person need! Women are natural helpers; men take care of your wives so your life can be long. The woman is your helper. Treasure your wife, let her feel important. Let your wife know that she is important. Women, you are your husband's helper, stop looking helter skelter! You are there to help him and God will reward you.

As a woman, you are a builder!

Proverbs 14:1: A wise woman buildeth her home! We need wisdom to build. You must know when to speak, when to keep quiet, when to comfort, when to build!

As a woman you are a servant!

Titus 2:4-5::These older women must train the younger women to love their husbands and their children to live wisely and be pure, to work in their homes, to do good, and to be submissive to their husbands. Then they will not bring shame in the Word of God. You are a cook, cleaner, laundry woman and nanny!

When last did you love him and lay his head on your chest? When last did you run up behind him and kiss him? Once a bride, always a bride.

Stop calling papa Joseph! Call him by a pet name. He is your husband. You are a servant, not a slave.

You are an intercessor!

Prayer cover him, Satan proof him, Delilah proof your husband, if God has blessed you with a husband, pray for him. The praying woman is a winning woman, at certain times, just pray for your husband! No matter how happy you are in your marriage, never stop praying for your husband. In case you do not know, some people are not happy that you are happy. That husband you think is useless, some people are queuing to marry him. Take care of your home, no matter where you go, come back to your home!

As a woman, you are a lover! Some women forget that they are a lover! Every man is attracted by what he sees, while a woman is attracted by what she hears. That is how we are wired! The male species like variety, even Christian men can be tempted! Therefore, you must be many things to your husband. Become unpredictable in marriage. Wear your hair differently, dress differently!

You should have two types of night wears; the general ones and the ones only your husband can see you in, you know what l mean. Look lovely for your husband, remind him of what he has. Make the room you share have a wonderful ambience!

Touch your husband! A woman needs thirteen (13) meaningful touches a day! Do not be an old ugly bride around your husband, work hard to retain your shape!

You must be romantic and spontaneous! Befriend your husband, if you do not befriend him, you will wake up one day and find a huge emotional gap! Do not let your ministry or career cause a rift between you.

As a woman you are a covering!

Look at Genesis 21:9-10.

What a man cannot see, a woman can see! So, as a man, learn to listen to your woman! Be careful when your wife warns you about a particular business or a friendship or woman, listen to her and try to understand her! Do not tell your wife to shut up. As a woman, protect your husband, defend him!

You are a keeper, an assignment

For example, he gives you sperm; you keep it, deliver a child and nurture that child. He tells you his vision, you keep it in mind and help nurture and bring it to pass. May the Lord give us understanding, Amen.

## GOD- GIVEN PURPOSES FOR SEXUAL INTIMACY IN MARRIAGE ARE:

1. **Unity**- Man shall be joined to his wife.

   **Genesis 2:24: Therefore shall a man leave his father and his mother, and shall cleave unto his wife: and they shall be one flesh.**

2. **Comfort-**Isaac took Rebecca, she became his wife and he loved her. So, Isaac was comforted after his mother's death.

   **Genesis 24:67: And Isaac brought her into his mother Sarah's tent, and took Rebekah, and she became his wife; and he loved her: and Isaac was comforted after his mother's death.**

   **Genesis 24:17: And the servant ran to meet her, and said, Let me, I pray thee, drink a little water of thy pitcher.**

3. **Procreation**- Then God blessed them, and God said to them, **Be fruitful and multiply (Genesis 1:28).**

4. **Defense-**A defense against temptation. Nevertheless, because of sexual immorality, let each man have his own wife, and let each woman have her own husband. Do not deprive one another except with consent for a time, so that Satan does not tempt you because of your lack of self control **(1 Corinthians 7:2,5).**

A husband is commanded to find satisfaction **(Proverbs 5:19)**, and joy **(Ecclesiastes 9:9)** with his wife and to concern himself with meeting her unique needs **(Deuteronomy 24:5; 1 Peter 3:7)**. A wife is responsible for availability **(1 Corinthians 7:3-5)**, preparation and planning **(Song of Solomon 4:9), interest (Song of Solomon 4:16; 5:2)**, and sensitivity to her husband's needs **(Genesis 24:6,7)**.

## SOME OF THE THINGS THAT ENHANCE INTIMACY IN MARRIAGE

### SLEEPING TOGETHER

Sleeping together is a must for every married couple.

It does not matter if you have fifty (50) rooms in your house, it does not matter if your children have a room for themselves, but it is very important that the couple sleep in the same bed in the same room.

The wife can have her own room where she keeps most of her belongings, female friends and family can sleep in the wife's room whenever they pay a visit.

Many couple sleep together only when they want to make love, and after having sex, they both go to their separate rooms. This habit is not good enough.

Don't sleep together only when you want to have sex.

When couple sleep together, they gist, talk, romance each other, all these things rekindle love and enhance intimacy between husband and wife.

Quarrel and pending unresolved matters can easily be attended to and resolved amicably when in the bed together.

Body contact of a couple is very important, everything is not about sex, when you sleep together you create awareness and bond.

Note this, when a couple sleep in separate rooms, they can both fall into temptation because there will be freedom to relate with the opposite sex which can lead to adultery.

## EATING TOGETHER

*Eating together is another thing that can bring intimacy between husband and wife.*

*Eat together at least once a day.*

*If possible eat together in the same plate, if not, eat at the same time.*

*Eating together as a family gives you a sense of belonging.*

*Wife, if your husband is likely to returen very late at night from work, you can take light food to suppress hunger till he comes back. Make sure you eat together at least once a day.*

## BATHING TOGETHER

Bathing together is fun. Bathing together is romantic.

Married couples should cultivate the habit of bathing together. This should be done regularly most especially at night when the children are asleep.

## GOOD COMMUNICATION

*Good communication is healthy for your marriage.*

*There is power in communication as it energizes the couple and also binds them together as one. Don't toy or fail to have good communication together often. By this, it shows you are both committed and your relationship is still alive funtioning. Communication is what takes your relationship to the next level. Any marriage that lost its communication lost its breath.*

## DATING

*Dating is not limited to singles alone. Married couples should find time to go on a date too.*

*You can fix a day out of your busy schedule to go out on a date.*

*This type of dating does not involve children, you go out with your spouse and have fun.*

*Going out on a date often can strengthen your love and your intimacy with your spouse.*

## *PLAY TOGETHER*

*You need to see your spouse as your best friend, feel free to relate and play together. Genesis 26:8*: **And it came to pass... that Abimelech King of the philistines looked out through the window and saw**, *and, behold, Isaac was Sporting (playing) with Rebekah his wife.*

Don't operate like Boss and employee.

You need to see yourself as one and as a playmate.

Don't be too serious to the point of not leaving a room to play together.

Watch movies together, read the Word of God together, share ideas together, play games together.

## PRAY TOGETHER

Couples that pray together stay together. When you hold hands and pray, you connect with your spouse spiritually and physically.

When you pray together, you speak with one voice, you agree together spiritually.

Praying together regularly can do signs and wonders in your marriage.

Our Marriage is Blessed.

## SEVEN SIMPLE THINGS THAT CAN BOND FAMILY TOGETHER DAILY

To increase the level of bonding in your family, the following simple things can help your family. They work for my family. They can work for your family too. Make sure you do one of them daily.

1. Pray together as a family. It does not have to be one (1) hour prayer meeting. But pray together as a family. It bonds family together.

2. Eat together: Almost everyday I buy something for the house. Once I get back home, I share it and we all eat it, sharing it together.

   'The Lord' Supper. This is different from our dinner. We also eat together as couple. If you have small children, let them eat together or at the same time. Food bonds people together very well.

3. Watch news, video or listen to songs together. It helps family to bond well. It increases family intimacy time.

4. Have your bath together. It might not be possible in the morning as you both might be rushing out of the house at different time. But in the night, take a shower together. We do that in my family. It helps us to gist, touch each other and the 'Act of all couples' can start fron that bathroom (not Act of apostles oo).

5. Do house chores together: Yes, it promotes intimacy in the family. It is like a family exercise.

6. Play together: Yes, there are small small plays you can play as couples. You can have couples' dance in your sitting room and ask your children to pick the best dancer between daddy and mummy. You can put down any amount and let the one the childern pick as the best dancer take the money.

7. Sex: It must be a normal norm in marriage. It bonds the husband and wife together and when daddy and mummy are well bonded, it promotes bonding in the entire family.

Apart from number one that is a must and should be a daily dose. You can pick anyone and do it each day, any day or every day.

So many factors are reducing and fighting family bonding times these days. We must make deliberate efforts to remain bonded as families.

You are not couples until you are coupled together and those tips I mentioned up there can couple couples and family together.

## BENEFITS OF MARRIAGE

1. **Divine Favour-Proverbs 18:22: Whoso findeth a wife findeth a good thing, and obtaineth favour of the Lord.**

2. **Fruit Of The Womb**

   **...They have a good reward for their labour (Ecclesiastes 4:9).** One of the rewards for marriage is the fruit of the womb. **The Bible says, Lo, children are an heritage of the LORD: and the fruit of the womb is his reward ( Psalm 127:3).** One of the reasons God created marriage is for procreation. God wants godly seeds within the context of marriage as stated in Malachi chapter 2. That was God's plan from the beginning **(Genesis 1:26-28).** The fall of Adam and Eve brought about barrenness. God sent His Son Jesus Christ to redeem mankind from every curse of the Law.

3. **Spiritual Power**

   It is expected for husband and wife to be spiritually stronger than when they were single. Two of them brought together in warfare against the devil, will cause ten thousand devils to flee **(Deuteronomy 32:30).** They become greater terror to the devil now than when they were single.

4. **Divine Security**

   And if one prevail against him, two shall withstand him; and a threefold cord is not quickly broken. **Ecclesiastes 4:12.**

   A three-fold cord is formed by God, the husband and the wife that will not be easily broken. As man adheres to God's precepts in marriage, God will honour the family and ensures nothing prevails against it. They (the man and the wife) are equipped to withstand, with the help of the Lord, all demonic forces and pressures of the world.

5. **Divine Presence**

   Again, if two lie together, then they have heat: but how can one be warm alone? **Ecclesiastes 4:11**. In the home where there is love, understanding and joy, God rewards it **with** His presence. **For in His presence is fullness of joy (Psalm 16:11).**

# CHAPTER FIVE

# Why Christians Remain Unmarried

1. **Misconceptions And Confusions About The Will Of God Or Perfect Match (Both Sides)**

   There is a whole spread of confusion in the body of Christ concerning marriage. Unbelievers, marriage is a contract not covenant. There seem to be sacrilegious in the body of Christ. Paul the Apostle for example was not married, yet he articulated a lot of things about marriage. Jesus was never married, but He said a lot of things about marriage. Marriage is a mystery, is not based on longevity, is based on the Holy Spirit. What exactly does the Bible teach about the Will of God?

2. **Unreasonable Standards And Expectations.**

   Unreasonable standards and expectations either from the guy or the lady. We are not against the standards, but when they are unreasonable.

   - Unreasonable expectation concerning financial status
   - Unreasonable expectation concerning levels of establishment.

   Do you have a car? Which type of house do you live?

   - Unreasonable expectations about physical appearance.

   The only person who can fit into those standards is Jesus Christ.

   Brothers, no lady that is enough. She must be this, tall, figure eight. When she smiles, she will have white teeth. There are many brothers who will never get married because they have unreasonable standards.

## 3. Difficulty In Early Establishment

This is Africa predicament, for example Nigeria. In Universities there are a lot of strikes. An average Nigerian can not guarantee for next twenty-five years, he will be established. High unemployment rate, difficult for many graduates to get employment. Poor salary payments have made it difficult for them to establish. Someone goes to School, University, after passing through the rigours and graduated, he cannot get gainful employment. In Africa, an average person has siblings to take care of. For those who want to start businesses, we have very stringent conditions. In Western world, for example, in England, you can register a Business in ten minutes on-line. In Nigeria, you can see a man of thirty or forty years still in the father's house single.

## 4. Ungodly Parental Influences

In Africa especially in Nigeria, there are ungodly parental influences.

- Geographical barriers
- Cultural barriers
- High marital requirements- unreasonable dowry requirements
- Influence of parents before and after marriage.

Some parents are desperate for their children to marry from a particular place.

It was easy for our parents because there was no migration, they live communal lives.

Some parents want their children to marry from their places whether the person is born again or not. Unreasonable marital requirements. Uncles, Aunts, who never contributed anything to you will now come and put a lot of things.

## 5. Increased breakdown in moral and spiritual standards

Degradation in morality and spirituality make them not to get married. Degradation in moral and spiritual standards.

Our generation has degraded morality, sleeping around, pre-marital sex.

Many people are not married, but living together. She has many men who provide for her financial needs. She has liberty. Degradation in moral and spiritual standards have created immorality.

## SOME CAVEATS TO GUIDE YOU AS A MAN

There must be quality decision to get married.

There is need to ensure some clear basics: House or accommodation. You need a good enough accommodation before you get married. It is demeaning for both of you to squat in a friend's house or your parents' house after marriage.

You must have a job or employment.

If you do not have a job as a man who will be the head of your family? Think twice before getting married. You should not get married no matter how much faith you have in God. WAIT. Your marriage should not start on a beggarly note; and should not glorify over- dependency. If your spouse has a job and you do not have, that could solve your problem. You have reversed the order. **The man is the bread winner, the hunter, the provider.** You have ceded your territory when you started making her the "provider". Later on, you will be challenged and you will complain of not getting enough respect; and being bossed by your wife, when house helps will tell you to your face, you are not paying their salaries.

In some cases, when a man feels not respected enough, he is usually driven to foolish escapades to assert his manhood, beating the woman, or brazenly taking another woman.

The man must be the head of the family even if he is disabled. He still is.

He may not have money; but in his mindset and emotional make up, and conscience, he should accept the honour, and exercise full responsibility as the head. He has no apology to make to the world, if he does not have all the wealth, the high status, and all the money because rich or poor, by God's and societal endorsement, he is the head and should behave accordingly with self respect and dignity. He is the cover for the woman and the family, and also the priest of the family. Every woman, no matter how big, no matter how much richer, yearns to have a real man beside and behind her who will be her human protection and shield. For instance, if there is a strange knock at the door, a woman expects her man to get up and go and check it out: or a snake crawls by, a woman expects a man to go after it. If he never does, and does not act like the head, there is always some depreciation of this man.

**A smart woman in courtship should detect how much of a man, her man wants to be; and if she detects a streak of irresponsibility, and a "drone**

syndrome", she should run away as fast as possible. **Women love their husbands to be their heroes**. Will this one be a hero: or will you for ever be missing a hero in your home, and may be one day blurt out your contempt for him and start fighting?

It takes a man to qualify as a woman's hero, and this recognition strengthens the home. A woman should also watch out for a dangerous streak which makes a man put himself and what he wants in the centre of everything; l am a traditional man; l like my wife to cook for me; and to serve me. I like my food warm- but not warmed up in the microwave. I do not want to sight any Okra seed in the soup; it must have been thoroughly blended. I like-, I do not want- - -". As you can see, such a man is the centre of the universe- you cannot satisfy his wants. He is narcissistic and your bickering and wrangling will cause a lot of tension in the home; and you woman will be full of resentment all the time in the home. Watch out how you deal with this suitor. If you are not ready to cope, go your way.

## WHEN MARRIAGE SHOULD NOT GO AHEAD IN ORDER TO AVOID AN UNHAPPY HOME

1. **Marrying For Pity**-You should not marry a man or a woman because you feel pity for him or her. A marriage is a contract not a charity. After all due considerations, and soul searching, and a conviction that there is a likelihood that you two can blend, fuse, or bond together, share together the responsibilities of bearing and raising children together, and by your good examples help them to become successful individuals, viable and safe citizens, you may decide to marry.

   You should never say to someone, "I did you a favour in marrying: you are too old"- or "I picked you up- you would have remained homeless". "You should be grateful". These were real statements made to female spouses.

   A marriage takes place when you are satisfied that both of you have what it takes to provide a home, a safe heaven where both of you will spend the rest of your life together and where the emotional atmosphere will be conducive for both the physical and emotional development of your children.

   Marriage is not what you walk into without courtship, which is the period of time you get to know each other. **For the very spiritual be warned.**

A marriage is likely to survive turbulence if your wife is your friend and if your husband is your friend. True friends do not hurt each other. True friends know everything about each other good or bad; and still love each other.

True friends are likely to share common interests or at any rate are likely to pick up the interest of their partner. For example: if one loves tennis, the other will also try to pick up interest in tennis, to enable them to go together.

True friends can be kneaded together both in the soul and in the body.

True friends can be friends and lovers thereby strengthening the bond in marriage through sexual intimacy.

The ingredient of friendship in the marriage puts a seal in the marriage and resilience for longevity.

This is because even if sex is no more a factor by reason of age or sickness, the bond of friendship holds the marriage together.

**You are therefore to be your wife's or husband's best friend and lover.**

The world can then see you are holding hands together and riding through the eye of the storms of life, and your home exuding hope, cheer, and joy: no matter how the weather of life is.

**In summary to this segment, do not marry for pity.**

If you want to help someone, do so other than through marriage.

You should marry as friends, coming into the union with mutual agreement and with your own personal assets to make the marriage work.

2. **You Do Not Marry For Fear**

Manifestation of quarrelsomeness in courtship is a dangerous signal. If hostility and quarrelsomeness constitute a trait in the spouse to be, it can signal strife and contentions in your home.

The causes of quarrelsomeness are short temper, selfishness, etc. An attitude of peace, and readiness to back down, mutual respect, cooperation, eagerness to please, and the heart that cares and forgives are gems to be looked for.

There is no doubt that rowdy, unruly fiancés should be carefully reconsidered. A short tempered, hostile and aggressive suitor should be dreaded. Resort to show violence, no matter for what cause, shows that this man can also beat his wife to be.

3. **The Quality of Empathy, Kindness, and Charity**

Meekness is forever to be treasured in a man because; he is a broken man who can be safe to live with in a home. Add to kindness, empathy and charity, you get a man in whom the spirit of God resides.

On the other hand, consider the opposite. Courtship can afford you the opportunity to watch out for signs of insensitivity and wickedness. If a man or a woman cannot hold out an argument, or a dialogue, but wants his way and his way only, this is dangerous. If you are not coming along with him, and he slams the door or pounds on the table to silence any attempt to thwart him, be warned. Those who always want to have their ways cannot be stopped. They can do anything even if it means hitting a woman. They may exhibit the following tendencies;

- Threaten
- Shout you down
- Stomp out
- Resort to violence
- End a conversation abruptly
- Withdrawing favours,
- Demanding change; but himself not willing to change.

These are all dangerous signs of traits that will cause strife in the home and may lead to battering.

4. **Hiding Secrets**

It is very wicked to hide secrets that can affect the peace, the reputation or the finances of the family after marriage such as:

- Criminal records
- Indebtedness
- Secret diseases
- Involvement in the occult

All these can affect the fortunes of the marriage and the home.

If you do not want any surprise later, be more vigilant in your courtship.

Intending spouses should be transparent or get ready for accusations or counter accusations of betrayal. **Tell him before he finds out! Tell her before she finds out!**

## THE MAN AND HOME-MAKING

A man's greatest asset is compassion. A woman and home should be safe with a man with compassion, and a forgiving heart; and a willingness to sacrifice- deny himself for the sake of you or a child.

So for you, woman, the greatest assets to look out for are **spiritual assets**, compassion, kind heart, generosity, magnanimity of heart which go beyond the expected, eager to please, protective, supportive, supremely responsible, available, and attentive.

**A man who loves God, fears God; and honours God in spirit and in truth is safe for you to marry and suitable to lead a happy home where God is FIRST.**

It is usually more difficult for men to become believers than women. It could be something to do with the male ego or male power, but it takes the average man a longer time to become a believer than the average woman. So, in every Bible- believing church, you are more likely to see more women than men. This means that many husbands are more tardy in coming on the train of believers than their wives. **So, it is indeed a blessing to have a suitor who is truly born again and truly a believer.**

An eligible man should be a believer and a worshipper. Otherwise, a woman has a problem in her hands, especially if you go ahead and marry him.

If your potential spouse is too cold about God, and you yoke with him, you have forged a partnership and union that unless your zeal for God will be over- compensatory, is headed for a collision with God or with Satan, that will be catastrophic. Simply, a home cannot do without God's help at all times.

# SERENDIPITIES TO REMEMBER ABOUT HOMES AND MARRIAGE

- Marriage is not a competition; it is a cooperation and blending.

- The home is not a battle front; it is a front for peace and succour.

- The home is not a hell on earth; it is a paradise on earth.

- Your spouse is not your greatest enemy; but your greatest and best friend.

- Your home is not a place to run from; but a place to run to.

- No marital problem has ever been solved by strife and fight; but by discussion and win-win solution.

# THINGS THAT MUST NOT HAPPEN BEFORE YOU DECIDE TO MARRY

1. **Financial Indebtedness:**

   Do not borrow from your fiancé so that if you pick up critical cues that suggest this marriage should not take place, you can be free to walk away.

2. **Pre-Marital Pregnancy:**

   You ought not to be pregnant before you decide to marry legally. Avoid this trap so you be free to walk away, if you hear from God or confirm cues that this marriage will not work.

3. **Pre-Marriage Co-habitation:**

   You ought never to be living together before you get legally married because, it will be difficult to pack up and leave if you become convinced that this marriage will not be a happy and successful one.

4. **Pre-Marriage Joint Investment:**

   You should not contrive any joint investment together nor any business deal for that matter, till you are convinced, and are ready to tie the nuptial knot. Otherwise, it will be messy trying to pull out of the deal if you become convinced that you ought not to marry this person. For instance you do not buy a house together till you are legally married.

5. **Pre-Marriage Procreation of Children:**

Nor indeed should you have a child together before you get legally married.

In all, do not jump the gun so that it will be easy to get away if you decide to do so. By all means avoid any form of entanglement or trap that may compel you to go into marriage in which you have already identified a potential threat, an irritant, or a pitfall in the anticipated marriage. Why walk into a problem, and then only to divorce? **Prevention of divorce is better than divorce.**

## WHY A WOMAN MUST NOT GET PREGNANT BEFORE MARRIAGE

A woman should not get pregnant before marriage not even for a month. If you do, you have jumped the gun.

It is a lie to stand before the altar for the blessing of the marriage when you have already gotten pregnant. Children are a heritage of the Lord, and God's reward to married people. Psalm 127:3-5. That is, God blesses the married people with children. It is important to wait and get blessed by God before getting pregnant.

It is a lie from hell that this man- the bridegroom-to-be, has to test you and ensure that you can get pregnant before taking you to the altar. If he does that, he is a presumptuous male, and probably not a Christian. Who said that it is a "must" that you should get pregnant as soon as you get married? Sometimes, you can; but at other times you may have to wait, sometimes one year, or two years or even more! A heavenly couple waits because God is a covenant- keeping God.

God has already blessed his people to be fruitful; and declared that nothing will be barren in the land of his people who fear him. Therefore, to impregnate a woman before the wedding to ensure she can get pregnant, is not only presumptuous, but a demonstration of unbelief and distrust of God.

Besides, if a woman gets pregnant before the wedding, she cannot escape if serious problems arise and suggest that the proposed marriage should not go on. She is therefore hooked! So by pre- marriage pregnancy, you can become forced into a marriage that is doomed to turbulence and disaster.

# MUST EVERYONE GET MARRIED?

1. No, for example, Jesus, His calling did not let Him get married, He died at the age of 33 years.

2. John the Baptist did not marry.

3. Apostle Paul – People that are gifted like Apostle Paul did not marry.

**First Corinthians 7:7: For I would that all men were even as I myself. But every man hath his proper gift of God, one after this manner, and another after that.**

There are people that are gifted that will not marry, they do not have sexual urge like most people. Celibacy is not for everyone.

## SIX VITAL SECRETS FOR A HAPPY MARRIAGE/ SECRETS OF A BLESSED MARRIAGE

There are secrets of blessings in marriage. The first secret is the knowledge of the reason for marriage. It takes great commitment for a marriage to succeed and be blissful.

1. Put God First in Everything.

   **The apostle Paul's counsel is, Whether therefore ye eat, or drink, or whatsoever ye do, do all to the glory of God (1 Corinthians 10:31).**

   **See also Matthew 6:33.**

2. Seek reconciliation at once.

   Remember love will not prevent misunderstandings or quarrels. Because we are human, seldom is husband or wife completely right or completely wrong. Any misunderstanding or quarrel should be settled immediately, on the same day they occur before going to bed at night."...**let not the sun go down upon your wrath (Ephesians 4:26)**. Be humble enough to say, "I was wrong" followed closely by "I am sorry."

James says, "Confess your faults one to another, and pray one for another (James 5:16). A successful marriage requires two sincere forgivers who can accept and forgive as God accepts and forgives us.

3. Be steadfast in love.

It is said that a successful marriage requires "falling in love many times BUT ALWAYS WITH THE SAME PERSON." The husband should love his wife with the same selfless and sacrificial love that Christ has so demonstrated on the Cross for His Church. The wife is to respond in the same manner. It is said that marriage is a two- way street of consideration and cooperation. It is founded upon kindness, selfless devotion and consideration. Great happiness is made up of little kindnesses. Lack of consideration and appreciation are great divisive factor in marriage. "Nag people and they sag; believe in people and they bloom." Another good reminder which l find very appropriate is from a poem from Margaret Sangster which runs like this:

We have careful thought for the stranger,

But often for our own,

The bitter tone,

Though we love our own the best.

4. Preserve The bond of Marriage

Preserve this unity at all costs. It is the gracious design of the Architect of marriage that the married couple remain faithful to each other and to God whatever the circumstances. **And they twain shall be one flesh: so then they are no more twain, but one flesh. What therefore God hath joined together, let not man put asunder (Mark 10:8, 9).**

5. Keep private matters private

The wedded couple should endeavour to keep certain matters to themselves and within the confines of their newly established home, "a sacred citadel of exclusiveness where no prying eyes or gossiping tongues are permitted." Even the Lord our God keeps His own secrets, but what He has revealed concerns us and our posterity (Deuteronomy 29:29).

6. Establish a mutual trust in money matters. Always keep in mind that whatever you possess comes from the loving hand of God. You are merely stewards entrusted with whatever God is pleased to bestow upon you. "But thou shalt remember the Lord thy God: for it is he that giveth the power to get wealth (Deuteronomy 8:18a). O.W. Toelke has some pertinent points pertaining to the management of family finances:

Most frequently, difficulties arise in the family finances when there is too great a disparity in the financial backgrounds of the marriage partners. Two people, even husband and wife, with different sets of financial values, and different attitudes toward money, can very readily disagree on how money is to be used. What one regards as a luxury, the other may consider a necessity.

In order to avoid difficulties in the administration of the family funds, some very basic concepts should be resolved upon at the very beginning of the marriage. Whether you are going to pool your resources in a joint bank account or keep a separate account, you know best and you need to come to an agreement from the outset. From my own experience, it is good to have a certain amount that one can use freely as one sees fit.

7. Mutual Submission. Mutual submission as believers in Christ. The Bible says in Ephesians 5:21: **Submitting yourselves one to another in the fear of God**.

1 Corinthians 7:3-4 explain further: **Let the husband render unto the wife due benevolence: and likewise also the wife unto the husband. The wife hath not power of her own body, but the husband: and likewise also the husband hath not power of his own body, but the wife.**

Another principle is the submission of the wife. The Christian wife must learn to submit to her husband. When she does, she receives blessings that money cannot buy:

**For after this manner in the old time the holy women also, who trusted in God, adorned themselves, being in subjection unto their own husbands. Even as Sarah obeyed Abraham, calling lord; whose daughters ye are, as long as ye do well, and are not afraid with any amazement (1 Peter 3:5-6).**

It is dangerous for a woman to go into a marriage with a man she would not willingly submit herself to; it is better that such a woman does not marry at all. When the Word **of** God says, **"Wives submit..."** Some people take it as a piece of advice rather than the express command it is, it must be obeyed. In fact, the

Bible goes further to reveal the degree of the submission, it says in Ephesians 5:24: "**...as the church is subject unto Christ, so let the wives be to their own husbands in everything.**

You would know a virtuous woman by the extend of her submission to her husband.

Proverbs 31:10: **Who can find a virtuous woman? For her price is far above rubies**.

## The Nature of Love

- Eros- Romantic Love- Essentially loving if loved in return. The world exists by this kind of love.

This is what lovers engage in, morally or immorally. This love is the lowest form of love, in that it is characterized by lust, conditions and the things both parties have to gain from one another.

In as much as this gain exists, the love continues. But when there is no benefit, then the love ceases to exist. They give terms and conditions to themselves on how far they can go. This type of love is commonly practised because it fits the world system. Sometimes we hear of align churches, nations and even communities, this is because of what they can gain from one another. But the Word of God says love seeketh not her own (1 Corinthians 13:5).

Our love should be demonstrated towards:

1. **God- Deuteronomy 6:5: And thou shalt love the LORD thy God with all thine heart, and with all thy soul, and with all thy might.** This love is why we use our time, talent and wealth to serve God. Loving God as a child of God is not negotiable, it is an integral part of our life.

   **Deuteronomy 30:6: And the LORD thy God will circumcise thine heart, and the heart of thy seed, to love the LORD thy God with all thine heart, and with all thy soul, that thou mayest live.**

2. **Our Neighbours- Galatians 5:14: For all the law is fulfilled in one word, even in this; Thou shalt love thy neighbour as thyself.** Our neighbours include our friends, enemies, strangers anyone that is a part of the human family. **Matthew 22:39, Leviticus 19:34, James 2:8, 19:11.**

3. **Nature** – The love for the environment God has given us, to protect and cherish it, not to destroy it.

4. Self- This is the love for one self. It prevents us from harming ourselves with dangerous weapons, drugs, e.t.c. Ephesians 5:29: **For no man ever yet hated his own flesh; but nourisheth and cherisheth it, even as the Lord the church**:

Matthew 22:39: **And the second is like unto it, Thou shalt love thy neighbour as thyself**.

- Phileo: Brotherly love, or being simply fond of one another.

This is the love amongst believers. This love encourages us to trust ourselves, as children of God pursuing the same goal – the kingdom. In this love, we are brothers and sisters in Christ. Same way you would not want to harm your biological family members, you would not want any harm to be done to your brothers in the faith.

David and Jonathan demonstrated this brotherly love as recorded in the following Scriptures.

(1 Samuel 18:1-4) **And it came to pass, when he had made an end of speaking unto Saul, that the soul of Jonathan was knit with the soul of David, and Jonathan loved him as his own soul. And Saul took him that day, and would let him go no more home to his father's house. Then Jonathan and David made a covenant, because he loved him as his own soul. And Jonathan stripped himself of the robe that was upon him, and gave it to David, and his garments, even to his sword, and to his bow, and to his girdle.**

Jonathan loved David as his own soul. This love does no harm, nor support destructive criticism. It was this love that made David, when he became King, to nourish Jonathan's son Mephibosheth (2 Samuel 9:6-7).

In Revelation, the Philadelphia church was commended for keeping His Word- (to love one another). Though with a little strength, love kept them on.

- Agape: Unconditional love, not with terms or conditions, not feelings, not erotic, not merely being fond of one another, but having fruit that resembles God's love (Gal. 5:22).

This is God's kind of love. It does not attach any condition or see faults. It is a kind of love lavished unconditionally. This is love that wants to give all, so that we can feel His love. Romans 5:8: But God commendeth his love toward us, in that, while we were yet sinners, Christ died for us. He loved us as we were. He didn't have to change us before loving us. When we were unlovable, He loved us without selection.

STORGE- Family Love

This is the love that exists between family members; father, mother, sons and daughters. It is the love that protects the family from external danger. Family members try to keep themselves safe and protected from outside influence and ridicule, even when a member, or members deviated from social norms and expectations. They defend themselves within the family, so as not to expose themselves to the public. If this love exists within the church, we would not wash our dirty linen in the public. We will protect one another irrespective of where we worship or belong.

Eros and Phileo are natural and okay in their places; man and woman should physically and mutually be attracted. Eros, the sexual, is part of the man's make- up. Phileo represents companionship. All three loves should be experienced by Christians. We do not get drunk with all kinds of feelings (Eph. 5:18), but filled with the Spirit. In this spirit, the husband is to respond to his wife as a matter of course. Agape is the highest of the loves and should be sought (1 Cor. 13:13).

Unity- The Central Principle of Marriage

Unity: The two shall be one flesh. One for all and all for one. Unity is the key (Eph. 5:31-32).

Reverence of wife: As the church is subject to Christ, so wives are subject to their husbands.

(1 Pet.3:2) She is to respect, defer, honour, esteem, admire, praise and be devoted to him. Above all, she is to encourage husband- never demean. Each is responsible to the Lord to change their respective lives to conform to godly principles regardless of the other's responses. By godly responses, we can influence, but only God has the authority and power to change the heart, the motives of another.

(1 Peter 3:6) Sarah recognized the Biblical view of marriage- the husband as head of a new unit. As head, he conveys to his wife by thought and by deed that she is valued, that he cannot do without her. She in return views her husband with great honour and

respect. Husband, above all else, is not to take his wife for granted. He is to convey to his wife, in spirit and in action, that she is "needed." Wife needs to know that she is needed in entirety, else sense of detachment and separation open the door to fear.

(Psalm 45:10) The wife formerly owed deference to her parents, now she owes it to her husband, but neither is to be controlled by their parents. The wife is never to be the head. However, decision making is to be coordinated. When Sarah called Abraham "lord", she recognized and honoured the authority which is of God. It is this God-given authority that she honours, not just the man only. She submits to him, to fulfil him, does not compete or strive with him.

Divorce: Individuality is stressed here. Two people are asserting their rights. The results are clashes, discord and separation.

Leaving, Cleaving, Weaving.

- (Eph. 5:33) Both husband and wife were in deference and submission to their respective parents. Now the husband must assume headship and the wife must defer to the husband. This is the beginning of a new unit. The parents are no longer to control them, but God is to be God. The parents are not to be God.

- (Col. 3:19) The husband is inclined to dominate. He is cautioned not to be harsh. If he is not harsh with himself, he will not be harsh with his wife as well.

- (Eph. 5:18) Do not be drunk with your own ideas, but be filled with the Spirit. A good place to start application of God's wisdom is in the home. As head of the home, the husband is not to abuse or misuse authority by being harsh or unkind or unfair. To act in this manner reveals the absence of the Spirit.

# CHAPTER SIX

# Why Marriages Fail?

1. **You must first love yourself**. Love your life so much now, and live your life and be happy. People have false expectations of marriage, when they get there, they are disappointed. Marriage is not going to solve your problem, solve your problems now and be happy. Self-love, not selfishness. Love yourself, love your life, pursue your purpose. If being married is going to be worse than where you are now, is better to remain single. When you marry, everything is going to be split; your time, your finances. You must have basic terms and conditions.

2. **People do not love each other**. A lot of people in marriage do not love each other. They love the word marriage, but do not love themselves. The Bible says, two must be better than one. If being married will be worse than where you are, do not marry.

## BASIC TERMS AND CONDITIONS

A. **Discuss sexual purity before you start dating**. Self-discipline is important.

B. **Who are his mentors?** Who are the people he is accountable to?

3. **People do not build themselves**. Everything you are supposed to do in marriage are things you do as a Christian.

A. **Forgiveness**

B. **Being Patient**

C. **Serving-** Serving another person. If everything is about you, you will not do well in marriage. Serve in church, examples: ushering department, choir department, sanctuary department, prayer warrior department and others. Do not marry someone for potentials, but marry for his patterns. Some marriages fail because of finances. Some have dreams, but never practicalize them.

4. **Be Honest**

A cheap way to disarm the devil is through obedience to the Scriptures. At the marriage in Cana of Galilee, when they ran out of wine, after telling Jesus about it, Mary said to the people, Whatsoever he saith unto you, do it. **John 2:1-9.**

Obedience turned their lack and impending shame into plenty and glory.

Do you want a happy and peaceful home? The Bible says:

**Wives, submit yourselves unto your own husbands, as unto the Lord.**

**For the husband is the head of wife, even as Christ is the head of the church: and He is the Saviour of the body.**

**Therefore as the church is subject unto Christ, so let the wives be to their own husbands in everything.**

**Husbands, love your wives, even as Christ also loved the church, and gave himself for it. Ephesians 5:22-25.**

Just obey these instructions and you will never need to pray for peace in your home.

## TEN RULES TO GUIDE YOUR MARRIAGE

1. Whenever there is an altercation or quarrelling, make sure you reconcile before going to bed. Always say you are sorry, kiss each other and make up. You never know when it will be your last time together.

2. Always take decisions together, whether big or small, good communication is a very important ingredient in marriage.

3. Do not say things belong to "me", like my car, my house, rather, say our car, our house even if they are yours, now you are one.

4. Always be courteous to each other. Treat each other with respect. Let each other know your whereabouts, drop notes if the other is not around, telling him/her where you have gone and when you will be back. It will be appreciated by the other partner/spouse.

5. Always say I love you at least once a day every day to each other.

6. Everybody has his/her own shortcomings or faults. Accept each other's faults, and manage them well. The Bible says, love covereth multitude of sin. Do not find faults with each other, instead give compliments to each other. Everybody loves compliments.

7. Accept each other's friends: even if you do not like them, pretend you do, and be courteous to them. Treat them with respect and kindness.

8. Be supportive to each other. Share each other's problems, his problems are your problems, and your problems are his problems. Fight it out together. Your husband's happiness/sadness is your own, and your wife's happiness/sadness is your own. Be supportive in each other's interests, develop interest in the things he/she likes. Encourage each other's vision, goal and aspiration. Two has become one.

9. Be Collaborative-Collaborate on projects for example, buying a house, car and so on. Whatever it is, work together.

   Working together on projects bring the family together.

10. Lastly, but not the least. Always kiss each other when parting, for example, going to work, and at night before going to bed. Make sure to say I love you before sleep over takes you.

# CONCLUSION

So many people are having problems in their marriages today because they were so desperate for marriage that they ended up marrying a devil.

Jacob was so desperate to marry Rachel that he did not study her character well enough to see her strong commitment to idols, and more importantly, he did not ask God to choose for him as had been custom in his family **(Genesis 24:12-14).**

You need God to enable you find the right partner.

**In Proverbs 18:22**, the Bible says:

**Whoso findeth a wife findeth a good thing, and obtaineth favour of the LORD.**

I pray for anyone trusting God for a future partner that you will find favour with God and know His Will. A sister should not agree to a marriage proposal just because she feels age is no longer on her side.

Only a man who is God- fearing and can love her as Christ loves the church is worthy of a sister's hand in marriage.

People say marriage is hard because they do not know the principles of marriage.

You must prepare for marriage. If you want to show a woman you love her, respect her.

Respect is reciprocal. You have to understand the love language of your wife. For men is submission. Women like surprises like gifts. Value your wife, buy her gifts, surprise her. Do not shout at your wife. We settle misunderstandings by talking. In your marriage God will never work on it for you, two of you must make it to work. The role of the Holy Spirit is He guides you. The Bible says, Blessed are the peace makers for they are the children of God.

Love is not enough to keep your marriage. One of the things that will keep your marriage is unity of purpose. Love is not enough, because there are a lot of imperfections, imperfections are shortcomings, but your convictions are what will keep your marriage.

When you know the weight of the assignment, forgiveness will be easy when you know your assignment.

The thing about marriage is that once you are in it, you cannot change your mind as God hates divorce **(Malachi 2:16).**

Brother/Sister, you need to be very sure that God is leading you into that marriage before you exchange those marital vows.

Do not marry someone for the sake of getting married. It is better to wait on God for the right person than to settle for just anyone because of societal pressures.

A lot of Christians who committed that error would tell you it is a grievous mistake to make.

An error in selecting a life partner could ruin a destiny. **The Bible says if the foundation be destroyed, what can the righteous do? (Psalm 11:3**). A word is enough for the wise.

Follow the Bible, live godly. Pray every day for your marriage. Your marriage will determine whether you will make heaven or not, because, there is no institution where you are tested as in marriage. If you have grudges or bitterness, Jesus comes, you will not make heaven. Is better you remain single than marrying a wrong person. God is a responsible father, He guides His Words. God will not tell you to marry a married man.

Do not base your marriage on feelings and love. You need a Word from God. As a man if you have prayed and you have a leading for a sister, carry your Pastor along. Do not let any man sleep with you until you are married. You can court for a short time and get married, than courting for a long time and fornicating. When you are in courtship, open up. Do not keep unnecessary details, tell yourselves about each other, explain each family member and how he/she behaves. Do not elope with anybody, do not get pregnant, get honour for your marriage. The man wants to visit the in-laws-to-be, dress well, do not over dress, if not they will over charge you. Be neat, be smart. Discuss intelligently with the man. When you are going, take little gift and give them. If there are children, take little money. Ladies, if you are going to meet your parents-in-law, do not dress in tight wears, or shorts, do not wear to expose your body, do not wear six inches shoes. When you enter, sit on the first seat, sit properly, turn only your eyes, not your head, try and be little shy. When everybody is speaking, shut up your mouth. If television is on, do not comment. If they ask you a question, just answer one word. If they serve you food, as a woman, do not finish it, make sure you do not spill your dress with oil. If you are eating with fork, do not full it, as soon as you finish eating, say thank you sir, thank you ma. Carry the plate to the kitchen and wash it, they will say this girl has home training. If you are going as a lady, do not take any gift because they will say you have come to bribe them.

Once as a lady you have been accepted, make sure you communicate with your in-laws without your fiancé knowing. When you are wedding, be careful who touches your hair. If you are going for your wedding, go to your Pastor to pray for you.

Generally, l do not say in sickness, in poverty.

I take thee as my wedded wife, in blessings, in health, together we stand against poverty, sickness.

Do not be indebted, live your life and believe God that all will be well.

The type of marriage we have chosen is the type of marriage ordained by God of Adam and Eve, one man joined to one woman, with God in their midst. This is Christian marriage which is contrived at the instance of God's expressed Will.

Therefore, this marriage should be conducted according to God's Way, and the home built according to God's Will. This is Heavenly Home, the home through which God will channel blessings to each of us; for God loves His families.

You cannot use the world's wisdom for God's wisdom or principles in marriage. Feminism will not work in marriage. The man is the head of the family, is the first, there is an order.

God is head of Christ, Christ is the head of church, and husband is the head of the wife.

We have dysfunctional marriage. Men and women are equal, worldly wisdom. You do not marry potentials, you marry patterns. Marriage is not created to make you happy, marriage will make you better. There is an order in marriage, husbands love your wives, wives submit to your husbands. Marriage has the ability to alter your life. There are sheep in wolf's clothing. Women, you should be fulfilled in life, when marriage comes, it is an addition. Irrespective of how good you are, if you marry rubbish, marriage will not work. If a man does not know how to deal with the wife with understanding, his prayer will not be answered. Prayer is the only weapon, "if you abide in me, and my words abide in you, ask whatever, l will do it unto you (John 15:7).

How can we abide in God?

Ecclesiastes 12:13 says: **Let us hear the conclusion of the whole matter: Fear God, and keep his commandments: for this is the whole duty of man. So then every one of us shall give account of himself to God** (Romans 14:12).

Pray for your husbands, stop fighting, stop nagging, prayer works. The heart of the king is in God's hands. God will throw it the way it pleases Him. Parenting is for two of you, if you are quarrelling, how can you parenting? The main reason for marriage is to complement each other.

The greatest marriage is found in Hosea 6, that is the marriage between the lamb and the church.

There are people who have not given their lives to Christ. There are others who have given themselves to the Lord, but backslidden. Please say this prayer after me:

> Lord Jesus, l come to You today.
> I am a sinner, I cannot help myself.
> Forgive me my sins. Cleanse me with Your precious blood.
> Cancel my name from the book of death, write my name in the book of life.
> Deliver me from sin and Satan, to serve the living God.
> Today, Lord Jesus, l accept You as my Lord, and my Saviour.
> Thank You Jesus for receiving me as a citizen of Your kingdom.
> Thank You Jesus, for saving me!

# ANOINTED BREAKTHROUGH PRAYERS

1. I revoke every witchcraft verdict in my marital life in the name of Jesus.

2. I smash into pieces every stronghold of the enemy in my life in Jesus' name.

3. Let all worshippers of idols prepared against my marriage die in Jesus' name.

4. Every enemy of my breakthrough, be consumed by the Holy Ghost fire in the name of Jesus.

5. Blood of Jesus, demolish every doorway of the enemy into my life in Jesus' name.

6. Father Lord, I destroy all the troublers of my marriage in Jesus' name.

7. All counsels against my marital life, collapse, in Jesus' name.

8. Every hidden enemy monitoring my progress, receive destruction in Jesus' name.

9. Any association between my husband/wife by any strange man/woman be scattered now, in Jesus' name.

10. Every curse that has been issued against my marriage, be cancelled in the name of Jesus.

11. Every legal ground in which my enemies are standing to attack me, be demolished in Jesus' name.

12. By the mercy of God, I silence my enemies permanently in the name of Jesus.

13. Every demonic mark contrary to settled homes, be wiped out with the blood of Jesus.

14. O Lord recreate my beauty to attract my God- given partner in the name of Jesus.

15. Let all evil in-laws receive angelic slap after the order of Herod, in Jesus' name.

16. I command the territorial spirits controlling me from my place of birth to release me in Jesus' name.

17. Father Lord, l refuse to be separated from my husband/wife in the name of Jesus.

18. Every demonic sacrifice offered against me and my marriage, be disgraced in Jesus' name.

19. O Lord! Arise and scatter all my stubborn enemies in Jesus' name.

20. Let all circles of marital problems break, in the name of Jesus.

21. I break every bondage of inherited marital failure upon my life and upon my marriage in the name of Jesus.

22. Any spirit or power manipulating spiritual children in my dream, die with your strange children in Jesus' name.

23. Every generational battle fashioned against my life shall not prosper in Jesus' name.

24. Every ancestral strange children transferred to me, l reject you by fire in the name of Jesus.

25. Father Lord, let all giants standing against peace and unity in my marriage fall down and die now in Jesus' name.

26. Let every power of the oppressors in my marriage rise up against each other in the name of Jesus.

27. Lord Jesus, let your power work mightily in every difficult situation in my marriage in the name of Jesus.

28. I command the arrows of the strongman working in my family to be roasted completely in the name of Jesus.

29. I paralyze all marriage destroyers and anti- marriage forces in the name of Jesus.

30. Let every pathway of witchcraft into my life be overturned by the blood of Jesus in the name of Jesus.

31. Any member of my family empowering external enemies, die by thunder in the name of Jesus.

32. Every arm of evil re- enforcement in my marriage, be scattered by fire of God and be roasted in Jesus' name.

33. l destroy all evil monitoring gadgets in my marriage in Jesus' name.

34. Let my wasters and my delayers in marriage be found no more after the order of Pharaoh.

35. I declare my ways open to victory over marriage in Jesus' name.

36. Blood of Jesus, silence every blood crying against my womb in Jesus' name.

37. Every curse placed against my womb, be destroyed now by the blood of Jesus.

38. Every evil covenant caging my womb, break in Jesus' name.

39. **(Hold your womb**) Every witchcraft altar in my womb challenging my pregnancy scatter.

40. **(Hold your womb)** Deposit of spiritual husband in my body be flushed out by the blood of Jesus.

41. You strange children calling me mummy, mummy in my dreams; l am not your mummy, die by fire, in Jesus' name.

42. By the Blood of Jesus, l erase every legal ground of the enemy against my bearing children.

43. My Father, my Father, By-pass all protocols and give me my children in Jesus' name.

44. l receive anointing for supernatural conception and miraculous delivery in Jesus' name, thank God for His divine healing.

45. Altars of darkness ministering barrenness against my womb, scatter by fire in Jesus' name.

46. Anything buried in the ground against my fruitfulness, be destroyed now by the power in the blood of Jesus.

47. Every negative prayer in my wedding or engagement day, that is negatively affecting my marriage, be nullified by the blood of Jesus.

48. You strange man in my dream claiming to be my husband, I am not your wife, die by fire in Jesus' name.

49. You wicked strongman that is always standing at my gate of miracles, enough is enough, fall down and die in Jesus' name.

50. You bondages of rising and falling operating in my father's house, by the power in the Blood of Jesus, I disconnect myself from you.

51. I will not go into wrong marriage in Jesus' name.

52. You satanic agent working against my marriage, fall down and die.

53. You spiritual husband, I bind you and cast you out of my marriage, in Jesus' name.

54. You spiritual wife, I bind you and cast you out of my marriage, in Jesus' name.

55. You serpentine spirit refusing me from getting married, fall down and die.

56. You evil hand diverting my blessings, wither and fall of, in Jesus' name.

57. I destroy every garment of rejection over my life by fire, in the name of Jesus.

58. Every strange woman against my marriage, be baptized with Holy Ghost fire.

59. I massacre every power working against my marriage with the sword of God, in the name of Jesus.

60. Every power that wants to make me to remain single, be roasted by fire, in the name of Jesus.

# ABOUT THE AUTHOR

Pastor Dr. Chi B. Okonkwo embraced Christ at a very young age. She comes from a very strong Christian background .She was a prayer warrior leader in Full Gospel Business Men's Fellowship International in the United States of America.

This international and non- denominational Fellowship was founded by an American Demos Shakarian of the blessed memory.

Dr. Chi loves the things of God and always committed to them.

She was ordained a Pastor in London by "World Union of Churches", worldwide, London Chapter, United Kingdom.

Dr. Chi studied in Poland, England and the United States of America.

During her studies in the United States, she emerged the best graduating student in her department in her graduating class, graduating with distinction with Summa Cum Laude, First-Class-Honours Degree.

As a result of this, she was a recipient of numerous accolades/awards - Departmental, University and National awards. This earned her the recognition of having her name published in the "National Dean's List of America", and, "Who Is Who", in America.

These two publications are national publications recognizing academically gifted students in America.

She holds a Bachelor of Arts, B.A. (Hons.), Summa Cum Laude, Master of Arts, M.A. (Hons.), Summa Cum Laude and Doctor of Philosophy, Ph.D. (Hons.), Summa Cum Laude, all from the United States of America ( U.S.A.).

Dr. Chi is very studious; she loves reading and writing which are some of her hobbies.

She comes from a privileged and academic background. Dr. Chi took her writing from her father, Chief Honourable Commissioner J.N.P. Okonkwo, a former Commissioner in Old Anambra State of Nigeria, University Lecturer, prolific writer, and author of numerous University text-books.

Writing runs in her family. These things are "in the blood!"

In Poland, she was the President of the Nigerian Students' Union, Sandomierz, Poland. In the United States of America, she was the Vice – President of the International Students' Association, Norfolk, Virginia, U.S.A., and at different times, the Vice- President and the Secretary- General of the Nigerian Students' Union, Norfolk, Virginia, U.S.A. Also, she was the Vice- President of the Nigerian Students' Union, New York, U.S.A. Dr. Chi was the Vice-President and Financial Secretary concurrently, Secretary- General and Social Secretary respectively of the Nigerian Nationals' Association, Madrid, Spain. She was the pioneer Secretary- General, and the Financial Secretary of Ohaneze Ndi-Igbo, Madrid, Spain, and, former Secretary- General of Anambra State Association, Madrid, Spain.

She was an Administrator, Lecturer and a Bank Manager.

Dr. Chi is a linguist; she speaks Spanish, Polish and English.

She is a member of the Association of Spanish Writers, and the first black woman and the first Nigerian woman to write in Spain.

Dr. Chi has authored several books. She is a published writer, an intellectual colossus and an erudite scholar.

**Other great books by Dr. Chi are:**

- The Efficacy Of Prayer
- Achieving Permanent Deliverance
- Unveiling The Hidden Secrets To Fulfilling Your Destiny
- The consequences of Disobedience/Sin
- Weak Women- Heroines
- Divine Favour
- Fighting For Justice

Printed in the United States
by Baker & Taylor Publisher Services